SUPPORTING QUALITY INFRASTRUCTURE IN DEVELOPING ASIA

JULY 2021

ADB

ASIAN DEVELOPMENT BANK

© 2021 Asian Development Bank
6 ADB Avenue, Mandaluyong City, 1550 Metro Manila, Philippines
Tel +63 2 8632 4444; Fax +63 2 8636 2444
www.adb.org

Some rights reserved. Published in 2021.

ISBN 978-92-9262-977-9 (print); 978-92-9262-978-6 (electronic); 978-92-9262-979-3 (ebook)
Publication Stock No. SPR210284
DOI: http://dx.doi.org/10.22617/SPR210284

The views expressed in this publication are those of the authors and do not necessarily reflect the views and policies of the Asian Development Bank (ADB) or its Board of Governors or the governments they represent.

ADB does not guarantee the accuracy of the data included in this publication and accepts no responsibility for any consequence of their use. The mention of specific companies or products of manufacturers does not imply that they are endorsed or recommended by ADB in preference to others of a similar nature that are not mentioned.

By making any designation of or reference to a particular territory or geographic area, or by using the term "country" in this document, ADB does not intend to make any judgments as to the legal or other status of any territory or area.

Please contact pubsmarketing@adb.org if you have questions or comments with respect to content, or if you wish to obtain copyright permission for your intended use that does not fall within these terms, or for permission to use the ADB logo.

Corrigenda to ADB publications may be found at http://www.adb.org/publications/corrigenda.

Note:
In this publication, "$" refers to United States dollars.

CONTENTS

Tables, Figures, and Boxes   iv

Foreword   vi

Acknowledgments   vii

Abbreviations   viii

Executive Summary   ix

1   The Impact of COVID-19 on Asia and the Pacific   1

2   Public Investment Efficiency in Infrastructure   9

3   Public Investment Management: Driver for Restoring   12
     Sustainable Economic Growth

4   Quality Infrastructure Investment: Knowledge Products, Tools,   22
     and the Infrastructure Governance Framework

5   Key Drivers of Quality Infrastructure: Efficiency, Accessibility,   25
     and Sustainability

6   Quality Infrastructure Investment: From Principles to Practice   27

7   Assessment and Performance of Quality Infrastructure Investment   48

TABLES, FIGURES, AND BOXES

Tables

1	Asian Development Outlook April 2021 Gross Domestic Product Growth Rate	2
2	Selected ADB Instruments Related to Quality Infrastructure Investment	46
3	ADB Corporate Results Framework, 2019–2024	49

Figures

1	Fiscal Balances Worsened and Debt Spiked across Much of Developing Asia	3
2	Policy Packages in Developing Asia	3
3	Results of Global Survey of Fiscal Recovery Policies	5
4	Impact of Global Push for Infrastructure Investment	10
5	Public Investment Efficiency Score by Region	13
6	Ranking of Public Investment Management Institutions by Scores in Design	14
7	Improving Public Investment Efficiency Could Increase Growth as Percent of Gross Domestic Product	15
8	Public Sector Investment Efficiency Varies by Income Levels	16
9	Worldwide Governance Indicator Regional Comparison (Estimates, 2018)	17
10	Public and Private Investment and State-owned Enterprises	18
11	Performance of State-owned Enterprises Relative to Private Firms	19
12	Real Growth by Forecast Year, 2019–2024	20
13	Debt–Gross Domestic Product Ratio by Forecast Year, 2019–2024	20
14	Growth of ADB Climate Financing 2011–2019 (including external cofinancing, $ million)	38
15	Internet Speeds and Wealth Index for Philippine Cities and Municipalities	41
16	Integrating Quality Infrastructure Investment into Upstream Policy and Project Cycle	44

Boxes

1   Asia and the Pacific: Progress in Mobilizing Domestic Revenues Set Back by COVID-19   7
2   International Monetary Fund on Fiscal Risks and Public–Private Partnerships   28
3   Using Big Data to Track the Pandemic   31
4   Moody's Methodology for Assessing Environmental, Social, and Governance   33
    in Credit Analysis
5   ADB: Promoting Climate and Disaster Resilience and Low-Carbon Development   34
    in COVID-19 Recovery
6   Principles of Climate Risk Management for Climate Proofing Projects   36
7   Samoa's Apia Port: Climate Resilience and Adaptation   37
8   Green Finance Strategies for Post COVID-19 Economic Recovery in Southeast Asia: 39
    Draft for Discussion
9   Sector-Wide Evaluation: ADB Energy Policy and Program, 2009–2019   40
10 Risk Allocation Reform and Creating More Collaborative Public–Private Partnerships   45
11 Evaluating ADB Support for Public–Private Partnerships (2009–2019)   47

FOREWORD

This report analyzes the importance of quality infrastructure governance, focusing on better understanding the constraints countries face across the investment cycle and the inefficiencies that undermine the value addition proposition. It identifies limited public investment management capacity as a constraint to reducing the infrastructure gap and ensuring the effective allocation of public resources to maximize the economic benefits of infrastructure investment. It supports the G20 Principles for Quality Infrastructure Investment to raise economic efficiency in view of life-cycle costs, build resilience against disasters, and strengthen infrastructure governance, while ensuring sound public finances.

The report fulfills two key objectives: (i) implementing quality infrastructure governance by improving the overall efficiency of infrastructure investment; and (ii) recognizing that the siloed, sectoral approach to infrastructure investment as traditionally practiced will not extend the life of an asset and sustain value addition.

The coronavirus disease (COVID-19) pandemic has presented a greater challenge to infrastructure development; countries now face even greater financing constraints to maintain infrastructure spending given competing demands on public finances. This challenge presents an opportunity to "build back better" and intensify efforts to ensure greater efficiencies in infrastructure investments. However, as countries embark on this roadmap, the objective will also target countries' own Sustainable Development Goals, and the returns on efficiency need to be integrated with parallel returns on inclusiveness and sustainability.

The report serves to initiate a dialogue on how the Asian Development Bank (ADB) can better support the efficiency of infrastructure investment in developing member countries for sustainable recovery and deliver key policy priorities, made more critical in a post-COVID context. Through this report, ADB seeks to contribute to the wider dialogue on quality infrastructure investment across multilateral and other development partners stemming from the Roundtable on Quality Infrastructure Investment held in Seoul, Republic of Korea in March 2019.

Woochong Um
Managing Director General
Asian Development Bank

ACKNOWLEDGMENTS

This report is led by Bruno Carrasco, director general concurrently chief compliance officer, Sustainable Development and Climate Change Department (SDCC); Hanif Rahemtulla, principal public management specialist, SDCC; and David Bloomgarden, lead governance specialist and Asian Development Bank (ADB) consultant.

The report has benefited from substantive inputs from Ramesh Subramaniam (director general, Southeast Asia Department [SERD]), Kenichi Yokohama (director general, South Asia Department), Srinivas Sampath (director, SERD), Aman Trana (director, Public Portfolio, and Financial Management Department [PPFD]), Jeffrey William Taylor (director, PPFD), Rana Hasan (director, Economic Research and Regional Cooperation Department), Robert Guild (chief sector officer, Sustainable Development and Climate Change Department (SDCC), Preety Bhandari (chief of climate change and disaster risk management thematic group concurrently director, SDCC), Yongping Zhai (chief of energy sector group, SDCC), John Versantvoort (head, Office of Anticorruption and Integrity), Trevor Lewis (advisor and head, Unit for Nonsovereign Operations, Strategy, Policy, and Partnerships Department [SPD]), Colin Gin (assistant general counsel, Office of the General Counsel), Almazbek Galiev (principal public–private partnership specialist, Central and West Asia Department), Shannon Cowlin (principal energy specialist, East Asia Department), Katherine Hughes (senior climate change specialist, SDCC), Smita Nakhooda (senior results management specialist, SPD), Belinda Hewitt (disaster risk management specialist, SDCC), Hyun Chang Park (public management specialist, SDCC), and Charles Andrew Rodgers (senior advisor, SDCC).

The authors are also grateful for all comments received from across ADB through interdepartmental circulation conducted in February 2021.

ABBREVIATIONS

ADB	Asian Development Bank
ADF	Asian Development Fund
CPS	country partnership strategy
DMC	developing member country
EPC	engineering, procurement, and contracting
ESG	environment, social, and governance
VFM or Vfm	value for money
G20	international forum for the governments and central bank governors for 19 countries and the European Union
GACAP	Governance and Anticorruption and Action Plan
GDP	gross domestic product
GIH	Global Infrastructure Hub
GRIS	green, resilient, inclusive, and sustainable
IDA	International Development Association
IFC	International Finance Corporation
IMF	International Monetary Fund
JICA	Japan International Cooperation Agency
LIDC	low-income and developing country
O&M	operation and maintenance
OECD	Organisation for Economic Co-operation and Development
PIM	public investment management
PIMA	public investment management assessments
PPP	public–private partnership
PRC	People's Republic of China
QII	quality infrastructure investment
RAMP	risk assessment and management plan
SDG	Sustainable Development Goal
SOE	state-owned enterprise
TA	technical assistance

EXECUTIVE SUMMARY

Introduction

Government policymakers face a substantial challenge in trying to address the extensive unmet needs for infrastructure services in many developing member countries (DMCs) of the Asian Development Bank (ADB). The report analyzes quality infrastructure in view of existing ADB instruments, programs, and projects. The intent is to promote dialogue on how ADB can more effectively support quality infrastructure in DMCs for sustainable economic recovery in the context of the post-pandemic coronavirus disease (COVID-19). The report balances conventional wisdom, emphasizing infrastructure financing and bankability, with a more encompassing approach that highlights governance and better integration of infrastructure systems including institutional development. It presents evidence that improving efficiency in infrastructure investment can contribute to greater volume and quality of infrastructure assets and service per unit of investment across DMCs.

Lower quality infrastructure investment and institutional weakness in planning, resource allocation, and project implementation can potentially undermine service delivery and even debt sustainability while failing to meet social, economic, and environmental objectives. The report unpacks the G20 Principles for Quality Infrastructure Investment in the context of ADB's programs and projects that promote improved infrastructure governance. It concludes with strategic recommendations to strengthen infrastructure governance, building on ADB strengths and capacities to implement ADB's Strategy 2030 operational priorities.

Impact of COVID-19 on Growth, Infrastructure, and the Sustainable Development Goals

This report promotes dialogue on how ADB can strengthen its support for quality infrastructure in DMCs to ensure a sustainable recovery and deliver key policy priorities in a post-COVID context. It assesses the impact of COVID-19 on growth, infrastructure, and the Sustainable Development Goals (SDGs) especially as the International Monetary Fund (IMF) labeled the current economic downturn caused as the "worst economic downturn since the Great Depression." The pandemic disrupted the construction, operation, and maintenance of infrastructure projects in countries around the world.

The *Asian Development Outlook* (ADO) *2021*, published in April 2021, projects that the combined gross domestic product (GDP) in the United States, euro area, and Japan will decrease by 4.8% in 2020 and expand by 5.3% in 2021. Developing Asia declined by 0.2% in 2020 and is expected to expand by 7.3% in 2021. Central banks in advanced economies have taken policy measures to provide liquidity and restore investor confidence. The ADB Brief, An Updated Assessment of the Economic Impact of COVID-19, estimates that economic losses in Asia and the Pacific could range from $1.7 trillion to $2.5 trillion under different containment scenarios; governments and international finance institutions have mobilized unprecedented funding in response.

Continued fiscal support is needed, but governments need to balance the need for infrastructure investment with the need for debt and fiscal sustainability. Governments have launched a large fiscal response to support health capacity, replace lost income incurred by households, and avert extensive bankruptcies. A growth rebound in 2021 spurred by low interest rates should help stabilize debt-to-GDP ratios. However, restoring sustainable fiscal balances will be crucial in economies that entered this crisis with low growth and high debt burdens. According to the World Bank publication Global Waves of Debt: Causes and Consequences in Finance and Development (2020), debt-to-GDP ratios have risen around 7% per year since 2010—almost three times faster than in the Latin American debt crisis of the 1970s. Though there is little evidence of this becoming a crisis, the pandemic will increase debt pressures in both advanced and developing countries. In 2020, fiscal deficits were more than five times higher in advanced economies and more than double in emerging market economies, leading to a significant increase in public debt of 26 and 7 percentage points of GDP, respectively.

COVID-19 has also slowed progress toward achieving the SDGs. With scarce public resources to address the public health crisis, ADB's DMCs are more constrained in delivering the quantity and quality of infrastructure investment needed to achieve the SDGs. According to the United Nations Economic and Social Commission for Asia and the Pacific (UNESCAP), even before the onset of the pandemic, the Asia and Pacific region was unlikely to achieve the SDGs by 2030. Despite significant progress on some goals like quality education (Goal 4), the region is likely to underperform on all 17 goals. In particular, the region needs to reverse trends on climate action (Goal 13), where it is sliding backwards.

Public Investment Efficiency: Driver for Restoring Sustainable Economic Growth

Section II of the report highlights the positive relationship between the efficiency of public investment in infrastructure and sustainable economic growth. Synchronized global investment in infrastructure could help lift growth domestically and abroad through trade linkages and enhance global output. The benefits of increased infrastructure investment are most impactful when interest rates and demand are low. According to the International Monetary Fund (IMF) publication, *Well Spent: How Strong Infrastructure Governance Can End Waste in Public Investment* (2020), public investments of one percentage point of GDP can increase output by about 0.2% in the same year and 0.5%, 4 years after the investment. The effects of public investment in the poorest countries are generally not as high, possibly due to lower investment efficiency.

Efficient public investment and stronger institutional capacity are critical to plan and deliver a pipeline of quality infrastructure projects. Public Investment Management Assessments (PIMAs) carried out by the IMF found that, on average, countries lose 30% of potential benefits of public investment in infrastructure due to investment process inefficiencies. Countries are better at designing public investment management institutions than managing them effectively. While many countries have formal national sector plans, they are often not properly costed out, not aligned with medium-term frameworks and annual budgets, and not used to inform public investment decisions. Although most countries have procedures to ensure transparent procurement, PIMAs showed procuring agencies were significantly noncompliant with those procedures.

Similarly, central monitoring of project implementation rarely results in corrective actions. While some countries have standardized technical criteria for project selection following international practices, governments often do not implement them. These apply to state-owned enterprises (SOEs) and traditional public agencies financing infrastructure. According to the World Bank report, Who Sponsors Infrastructure Projects? Disentangling Public and Private Contributions (2019), public sector investment, including investment by government entities and SOEs, account for 83% of infrastructure project investments in DMCs. Of this, 66% comes from SOEs and

34% from public agencies. Only 17% of total infrastructure investment is from the private sector through public–private partnerships (PPPs). SOEs accounted for 74% of total infrastructure investment in East Asia and the Pacific, with the People's Republic of China (PRC) accounting for 60% of the total and South Asia 44%.

Quality of Infrastructure Investment: From Principles to Practice

Section III discusses the relevance of G20 Principles for Quality Infrastructure Investment (QII) to ADB's diagnostic tools and its support to DMCs. The G20 affirmed the call for quality infrastructure by endorsing the Principles for Quality Infrastructure Investment at the G20 Finance Ministers' and the Central Bank Governors' meetings in Fukuoka, Japan (8-9 June 2019). The G20 communiqué called to maximize infrastructure's positive impact to achieve sustainable growth and development while preserving public finance sustainability, raising economic efficiency in view of life-cycle costs, integrating environmental and social considerations including women's economic empowerment, building resilience against natural hazards and other risks, and strengthening infrastructure governance. The Asian Development Fund (ADF) 13th replenishment and the International Development Association (IDA) 19th replenishment highlight the importance of the quantity and the quality of infrastructure investment in maximizing its development impact.

Efficiency, accessibility, and sustainability are key in operationalizing QII. Efficiency requires a project selection process maximizing social and economic benefits. The value for money (VfM) assessment, for example, measures social, environmental, and economic benefits in PPPs versus traditional investments. Accessibility is based on ensuring that infrastructure design and associated services are of high quality and accessible to all, including poor and marginalized communities, while directly consulting with these communities to ensure appropriate responses to their needs. Sustainability is based on extending the life of infrastructure assets, considering fiscal, economic, technological, environmental, social, and governance in line with the 2030 Agenda for Sustainable Development and the Paris Agreement to reduce greenhouse gases, and with countries' national and local development strategies.

To achieve quality infrastructure, ADB will need to reinforce its programs and projects to strengthen DMC infrastructure governance—the public institutions, processes, and procedures that guide government decisions in planning, allocating funds, and implementing public investment projects. Quality infrastructure is necessary regardless of the transactional mode; it may be achieved through full PPPs, traditional investment models, or the various models of PPP procurement. Infrastructure governance covers the entire life-cycle of assets, but the most resource-intensive activities are typically planning and decision-making. ADB needs to strengthen its ongoing support for the upstream policy and regulatory environment and the midstream infrastructure project cycle, aligning with the new ADB procurement framework and strategic procurement planning.

ADB has made good progress in implementing safeguards and results frameworks and moving toward quality infrastructure, but more remains to be done. Based on recent sector evaluations for PPPs and the energy sector, ADB needs more focus on upstream activities to support enabling environments, capacity development, and sector planning. It should develop a roadmap by working across departments to identify and select priority activities in each infrastructure sector, engaging with DMCs through high-level planning, policy design, and effective institutional reform and capacity building in project development. ADB can leverage its regional competitive advantage, financial resources, and policy dialogue to promote long-term infrastructure planning and public sector management capacity, generating higher impact investment opportunities. This will be particularly important in a post-COVID-19 world, where DMCs will need support to strengthen their economies. Debt and fiscal challenges will become more prominent in the face of natural hazards, COVID-19, and other epidemics.

Quality infrastructure is relevant to all aspects of Strategy 2030, especially in Operational Priority 3 (OP3), tackling climate change, building climate and disaster resilience, and enhancing environmental sustainability; Operational Priority 6 (OP6), strengthening governance and institutional capacity; and Operational Priority 7 (OP7), increasing regional cooperation and integration, and in particular, its first pillar for greater and higher-quality connectivity between economies. To address infrastructure governance, the report recommends a greater focus on upstream and midstream technical assistance (TA) to support the key drivers of quality infrastructure such as economic efficiency, life-cycle costs, and VfM. ADB already includes environmental and social sustainability, green investment, and building climate and disaster resilience under Strategy 2030. ADB should strengthen its coordination and collaboration with partners like the IMF, the Japan International Cooperation Agency (JICA) and other bilateral development partners, the Organisation for Economic Co-operation and Development (OECD), and the World Bank, especially on infrastructure assessment tools and knowledge sharing.

The report notes that quality infrastructure will require a relatively high level of sophistication in government contracting authorities that plan, procure, and manage infrastructure projects, as well as strengthened collaboration among thematic groups, departments with relevant knowledge, and regional departments within ADB. In addition, it requires that government fiscal authorities have the capacity to perform more refined calculations of liabilities and other contingencies to assess the cost of project risks and to establish a consistent methodology for making VfM and life-cycle costings and assessments. The high level of governance capacity needed in DMCs presents both a challenge and an opportunity for multilateral and bilateral development agencies. Transparency and accountability remain critically important, but these objectives can only be attained by strengthening the ability of contracting agencies to understand how to improve infrastructure governance.

To do this, ADB needs to coordinate TA and capacity-building programs among finance officials and infrastructure line ministries, including PPP units. Multilateral and ADB support is critical as a counterpart to transactional support in capacity building, with ADB upstream support in building local capacity not being a one-time operation. A recent ADB evaluation, ADB Support for Public–Private Partnerships (2009–2019), by the Independent Evaluation Office, showed the importance of a "One ADB" approach, with close coordination and feedback loops between the transaction experience and upstream and midstream policy and capacity building. The infrastructure, private sector, governance, and procurement departments within ADB will need to work together, coordinating and intensifying existing collaboration and knowledge sharing, to help contracting authorities develop the requisite skills, especially since government officials change across administrations and new ideas and priorities emerge.

The report provides recommendations to further strengthen ADB's support for quality infrastructure governance in DMCs leading to sustainable recovery and the ability to deliver on key policy priorities, made more critical in a post-COVID-19 context.

⊙ **Adopting a "One ADB" approach to quality infrastructure:** ADB's Strategy 2030 recognizes the thematic approach. The focus now should be on integrating sector work into themes and ensuring cross-cutting initiatives. Quality infrastructure requires expertise and knowledge in a range of areas across the institution to address complex and cross-cutting governance and development challenges, and to develop integrated solutions. To assist DMCs in developing the needed levels of governance capacity, ADB needs to ensure that its TA programs—for traditional infrastructure and PPP units, finance officials, procurement authorities, and infrastructure line ministries—are closely linked. Bridging internal departments of development agencies will be critical in developing a more collaborative approach to infrastructure investment.

- **Embedding infrastructure governance in the country partnership strategy:** Infrastructure projects are complex, requiring upstream planning, project prioritization, sound frameworks for procurement of traditional and PPP projects, institutional capacities for public financial management and governance, and a sound business and policy environment. An integrated infrastructure governance diagnostic assessment at the country partnership strategy (CPS) level is required for maximum impact. This should be guided by infrastructure governance for ADB to prepare a strategic long-term vision for infrastructure and sector-based policies in DMCs. It should address infrastructure governance in an integrated fashion where authorities plan, procure, deliver, fund, and finance long-term, fiscally sustainable infrastructure. It should consider transparency, stakeholder participation, and capacity to manage threats to integrity, drawing on existing ADB knowledge and developing infrastructure governance diagnostic tools in the country dialogue.

- **Integrating ADB diagnostic instruments:** Infrastructure investment is characterized by increasing levels of complexity to meet different objectives and deliver multiple benefits in the short and long term, all within the context of increasingly interconnected and interdependent infrastructure systems across geographies, sectors, and levels of government. ADB has an array of instruments and filters corresponding to infrastructure governance. The challenge is to integrate stand-alone instruments in a cohesive manner to address economic, social, fiscal, environmental, and climate-related costs and benefits, and to account for the full life-cycle of infrastructure assets. Country diagnostic assessments need to be refined and tailored to meet country circumstances in order to implement infrastructure governance in alignment with national-level policy and long-term development goals.

- **Embracing programmatic approaches to infrastructure governance at national and subnational levels:** ADB should build on programmatic approaches to support reforms through policy- and results-based lending in support of smaller scale investments and infrastructure investment projects. The ability of DMCs to identify and manage infrastructure risks at the institutional level, especially in subnational entities, needs to be strengthened. As national-level support for subnational infrastructure investment plays a critical role in investing in sustainable and resilient infrastructure, all levels of government should coordinate with institutions to ensure timely investment to support post COVID-19 recovery while ensuring the quality of these investments. This requires improved capacity within DMCs to monitor and evaluate infrastructure governance at the intermediate levels of government—regions, states, provinces—and should be part of national investment recovery strategies and dialogue with country authorities in preparing an ADB CPS.

- **Upstream and midstream support to improve infrastructure governance:** The Independent Evaluation Office's reports on both PPPs and the energy sector show that VfM across the life-cycle of infrastructure assets requires greater focus on upstream and midstream institutional capacity to strengthen public investment efficiency. In providing TA to build capacity in DMCs, ADB should focus more on upstream and midstream planning, project selection, preparation, and fiscal and debt management, plus downstream monitoring and evaluation.

  This includes supporting DMCs to adopt the necessary policy and regulatory frameworks that provide enabling conditions, incentives, and standards to promote sustainable infrastructure investment. It also means ensuring strong governance mechanisms, so the right infrastructure is built cost effectively and affordably, while engendering trust from stakeholders. Capacity-building support for infrastructure governance needs more integrated and holistic support across ministries for planning, selecting projects, budgeting, and managing infrastructure contracts and risks. It also requires systemic engagement and capacity building beyond a single project. Moreover, infrastructure investment depends on fiscal authorities' capacity to implement sound public financial management to ensure fiscal and debt sustainability. This means ensuring that authorities align plans with budget allocations in medium-term expenditure frameworks. A robust, transparent, and accountable capital budgeting framework helps build trust in government and meet national development needs cost-effectively and coherently.

○ **Mobilizing private finance through risk sharing and mitigation:** Financing for quality, sustainable infrastructure needs to be scaled up to support strong, inclusive, and green recovery from the COVID-19 crisis. Given increasing budget pressures, governments need to mobilize private finance to complement public investment. To broaden the investor base, appropriate capital market instruments and vehicles for channeling financing for infrastructure projects must be available so institutional investors can invest without undue regulatory constraints. Risk perception by institutional investors in a post-COVID-19 world is likely to continue given the increased debt and fiscal pressure, especially in poorer countries as the perception of policy, regulatory, and institutional risks limit the extent of institutional investment in DMCs.

Carefully calibrated government intervention can influence the overall level of risk, by managing environmental and social risks and promoting diversified risk mitigation instruments and incentives. ADB addresses this by using private sector resources for PPPs and providing specialized infrastructure financial products like blended finance, equity, and guarantees. ADB's commitment to climate financing and innovative green bonds strengthens the financing market for such investments. Expanding private finance by mitigating public and private stakeholder risks and enhancing policy dialogue with DMCs and the private sector to improve infrastructure governance are essential in meeting strategic investment needs. ADB can help increase private finance by promoting infrastructure as an asset class—for example, by improving DMCs' ability to measure and maintain data on the historical performance of infrastructure assets.

○ **Infrastructure governance and PPPs:** Countries need to improve the oversight of investment projects and PPPs and integrate economic efficiency, environmental and social sustainability, adaption, and resiliency in the operational framework for sustainable infrastructure development. The thematic PPP evaluation found that ADB's PPP operational plan did not have clear performance measures and lacked a focus on promoting advocacy, capacity development, and the PPP enabling environment.

Upstream work was found to mainly focus on sovereign interventions through policy-based loans and TA projects promoting advocacy, capacity development, and targeted support for the PPP enabling environment. Effective infrastructure governance also requires looking beyond the planning and prioritization process and ensuring that infrastructure lasts over the asset life-cycle. This requires monitoring strategies, paying due consideration to the operation and maintenance of infrastructure assets, and fostering investments to reinforce resilience of infrastructure systems. Strengthening the governance and performance of economic regulators also supports the market efficiency, quality, reliability, and affordability of private infrastructure services, and ensures the provision of critical infrastructure services following COVID-19.

○ **Using technology and innovation to improve infrastructure governance:** The infrastructure sector is lagging behind other sectors in the adaptation and implementation of innovative technologies. Artificial intelligence or machine learning can pave the way for smart city technologies by making transportation more intelligent and energy efficient. Big data can monitor the pandemic's impact on traffic patterns and transport patterns. Technology can also improve infrastructure governance. Digital technologies can operate in real time to support better governance and discipline, monitoring progress and troubleshooting mechanisms. It can also facilitate e-procurement systems including contract monitoring and recording for contractor and consultant registration systems.

The SOURCE software platform, for example, serves as a repository of the latest tools and diagnostics related to infrastructure project preparation and can disseminate ADB tools, safeguards, and other knowledge products related to improving infrastructure governance. This multilateral development bank-led digital project preparation software initiative is designed to improve project quality based on international best practices and was developed in consultation with user governments, multilateral development banks, and the private sector. Making relevant ADB tools and diagnostics more widely accessible to DMCs can promote interest and understanding of issues around infrastructure governance. Demand for ADB technical assistance from DMCs may also increase to support implementation of these tools and knowledge products.

○ **Collaboration with development partners:** Infrastructure governance depends on country leadership and policy vision to improve the efficiency of how DMCs identify, plan, design, and allocate resources for infrastructure projects. ADB can expand existing collaboration with the IMF, for example, to conduct PIMA diagnostics to identify infrastructure governance gaps. Building a common understanding of the importance of infrastructure governance among decision makers is necessary in its successful implementation.

The IMF, Organisation for Economic Co-operation and Development (OECD), World Bank, Japan International Cooperation Agency (JICA), and other international organizations are crucial ADB partners in improving DMC understanding and implementation of sustainable, low-carbon, inclusive, quality infrastructure objectives. Cofinancing from partners can also help alleviate initial costs of implementing infrastructure governance borne by DMCs. The various departments within multilateral and bilateral development agencies which deal with infrastructure, private sector development, governance, and public procurement will also need to work together, coordinating and intensifying their existing programs, to help governments in emerging and developing markets acquire the requisite skills.

SECTION

1

THE IMPACT OF COVID-19 ON ASIA AND THE PACIFIC

The coronavirus disease (COVID-19) has disrupted the construction, operation, and maintenance of infrastructure projects in countries around the world. The International Monetary Fund (IMF) has labeled this economic downturn the "worst economic downturn since the Great Depression."[1] The IMF *World Economic Outlook Update* for 2020 characterized the pandemic as a "crisis like no other, an uncertain recovery." The *Asian Development Outlook* (ADO) *2021* projects that combined gross domestic product (GDP) in the United States, euro area, and Japan will decrease by 4.8% in 2020 and expand by 5.3% in 2021.[2]

Central banks in advanced economies have taken policy measures to provide liquidity and restore investor confidence. In many Asian Development Bank (ADB) developing member countries (DMCs), central banks have relaxed monetary policy and provided fiscal support far exceeding those enacted during the 2008–2009 financial crisis. In addition, governments have mandated mitigation measures such as lockdowns and restrictions on travel to reduce COVID-19 infection and ease the stress on health systems. All these have curbed consumption and investment, disrupted production, and impacted global trade, supply chains, travel, and tourism.

The *ADO 2021* reports that developing Asia will contract by 0.2% in 2021. Table 1 shows that growth will rebound to 7.3% in 2021, but GDP will continue below its pre-pandemic trend. The restrictions on economic activities needed to address the pandemic have triggered recessions across advanced, emerging, and developing economies. This has lowered investment, eroded human capital, and disrupted supply chains (footnote 2). ADB estimates that the Asia and Pacific region could suffer losses from $1.7 trillion to $2.5 trillion under different containment scenarios.[3] In response, governments and international finance institutions have provided unprecedented funding of at least $10 trillion. ADB is helping DMCs respond to the immediate impacts of COVID-19 through an initial $20 billion response package (footnote 3).

---

[1] Gopinath, G. 2020. The Great Lockdown: Worst Economic Downturn Since the Great Depression. IMFBlog. 14 April. https://blogs.imf.org/2020/04/14/the-great-lockdown-worst-economic-downturn-since-the-great-depression.

[2] Asian Development Bank (ADB). 2021. Asian Development Outlook 2021: Financing a Green and Inclusive Recovery. April.

[3] ADB. 2020. Updated Assessment of the Potential Economic Impact of COVID-19. *ADB Briefs*. May. Manila.

Table 1: Asian Development Outlook April 2021 Gross Domestic Product Growth Rate

	2019	2020	2021
Central Asia	4.9	−1.9	3.4
East Asia	5.3	1.8	7.4
South Asia	4.2	−6.0	9.5
Southeast Asia	4.4	−4.0	4.4
The Pacific	4.3	−5.8	1.4
Developing Asia	5.0	−0.2	7.3
Developing Asia Excluding NIEs[a]	5.5	−0.0	7.7

NIEs = newly industrialized economies.
a   Includes Hong Kong, China; the People's Republic of China; the Republic of Korea; Singapore; and Taipei,China.
Source: Asian Development Outlook database; ADB April 2021 estimates.

Throughout Asia and the Pacific, the economic slowdown has contributed to delays in infrastructure financed as traditional public sector projects and by public–private partnerships (PPPs). Airports, for example, provide a grim picture of revenues for 2020, with a 50% drop in total passenger traffic (to 4.6 billion) and nearly 57% in airport revenues (to $97.4 billion), compared to pre-COVID-19 forecasts. A 58.9% drop in revenues from pre-pandemic levels in the Asia and Pacific region in 2020 was forecast by the International Finance Corporation (IFC) in May 2020 (footnote 3).

In order to respond to the immediate challenge, governments will have to reallocate spending requirements and reduce spending. Although infrastructure investment has been useful in stimulating growth, the impact of COVID-19 will reduce capacity to fund infrastructure from government budgets due to lower revenues. While increased infrastructure spending will help stimulate economic recovery in some countries, other countries may not be able to provide enough fiscal support due to their debt and revenue positions leading to reduced infrastructure investment or prioritizing spending on more immediate needs.

Governments need to balance infrastructure investment with the need for debt and fiscal sustainability though the top priorities are public health and the need for continued fiscal support. Governments have launched a large fiscal response to address capacity in the health sector, provide income support to households, and avert mass bankruptcies. A rebound in growth in 2021 spurred by low interest rates should help stabilize debt-to-GDP ratios, but ensuring sustainable fiscal balances will be necessary for countries with elevated debt and low growth.

The ability of governments to fulfill infrastructure needs will be stressed, especially in low-income countries, given the collapse in economic activity and revenues and the expansion of other spending needs—most notably social support and health spending. Figures 1 and 2 show the increase in public deficits and debt because of the economic contraction and the increase in policy support, with governments spending about 8% of GDP on income support. There is much less room for public infrastructure spending, and countries need strong debt-management capacity. Indonesia, for instance, has issued (domestic or international) bonds, including a pandemic bond for $4.3 billion, to respond to the COVID-19 crisis and support economic recovery. Prior sound fiscal and debt management capacity has made this possible with a deficit under 3% and a debt-to-GDP ratio around 30%.[4]

---

4   R. Assi et al. 2020. Closing the $30 Trillion Gap: Acting Now to Manage Fiscal Deficits During and Beyond the COVID-19 Crisis. *McKinsey Insights*. 16 July. https://www.mckinsey.com/industries/public-and-social-sector/our-insights/closing-the-30-trillion-gap-acting-now-to-manage-fiscal-deficits-during-and-beyond-the-covid-19-crisis#.

Figure 1: Fiscal Balances Worsened and Debt Spiked across Much of Developing Asia

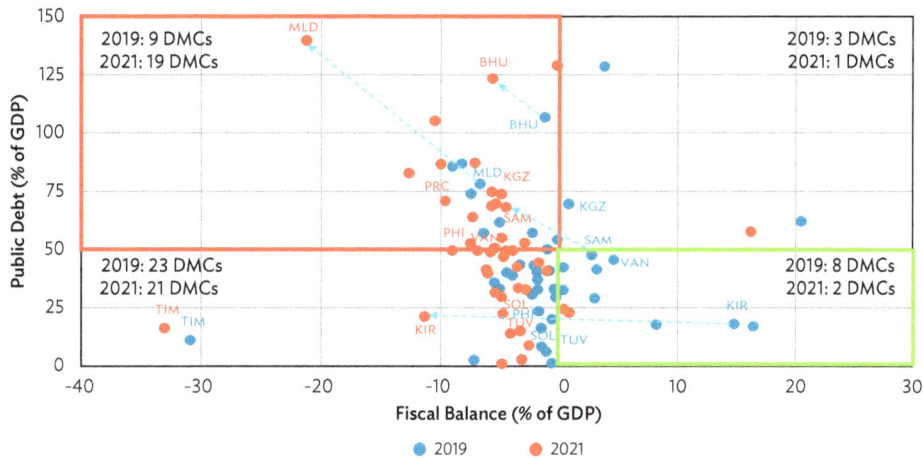

ADB = Asian Development Bank, BHU = Bhutan, DMC = developoing member country, GDP = gross domestic product, KGZ = Kyrgyz Republic, KIR = Kiribati, MLD = Maldives, PHI = Philippines, PRC = People's Republic of China, SAM = Samoa, SOL = Solomon Islands, TIM = Timor-Leste, TUV = Tuvalu, VAN = Vanuatu.

Notes: Projections are from Baseline Scenario. Comprises a panel of 43 ADB DMCs. Lower-income DMCs are shown with labels.

Source: DB projections using data from World Economic Outlook (WEO) April 2021 and Asian Development Outlook 2021 (April 2021).

Figure 2: Policy Packages in Developing Asia

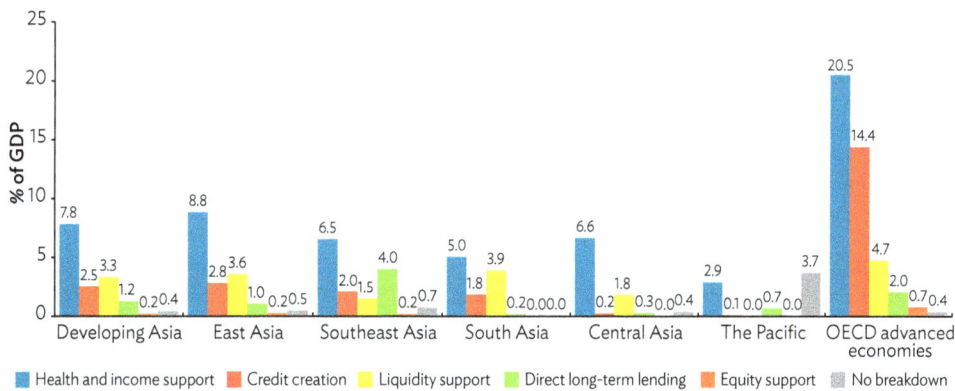

GDP = gross domestic product, OECD = Organisation for Economic Co-operation and Development.

Notes: Advanced economies include Australia, Austria, Belgium, Canada, Denmark, Finland, France, Germany, Ireland, Italy, Japan, Luxembourg, the Netherlands, New Zealand, Norway, Portugal, Spain, Sweden, Switzerland, the United Kingdom, and the United States. Data as of 28 June 2021.

Source: Compiled from ADB COVID-19 Policy Database. https://covid19policy.adb.org/ (accessed 5 July 2021).

COVID-19 has also decelerated progress in achieving the United Nations Sustainable Development Goals (SDGs). With scarce public resources channeled toward addressing the current public health crisis, DMCs have become even more constrained in delivering the infrastructure investment needed to achieve the SDGs.

The pandemic affects the most vulnerable, especially in densely populated informal settlements and slums. However, progress in reducing slum populations has slowed in some regions.

Even before the onset of the pandemic, the Asia and the Pacific region was not well-positioned to achieve the SDGs by 2030. According to the United Nations Economic and Social Commission for Asia and the Pacific (UNESCAP), income inequality, measured by the Gini coefficient, increased by over 5% between 1990 and 2014.[5] Close to 80% of the Asia and Pacific population live in countries with widening inequality (as measured by Gini coefficients).[6] Despite significant progress on some goals, such as quality education (Goal 4), the region is likely to underperform on all the 17 goals by 2030. In particular, the region is sliding backwards and needs to reverse trends on climate action (Goal 13). Globally, current emission reduction commitments are insufficient and would lead to a 3.2°C rise in temperature this century—well above the Paris Agreement target of 1.5°C.[7] The Asia and Pacific region emits half of the global greenhouse gas emissions, with the number doubling since 2000. The region's share of renewable energy as a percentage of total final energy consumption has dropped from 23% in 2000 to 16% in 2016, one of the lowest rates among world regions. In 2018, natural hazards affected the livelihoods of 24 million people in Asia and the Pacific.[8]

Global poverty rates are rising for the first time since 1998 due to the pandemic. The April 2021 ADO shows that poverty would have continued its decline in developing Asia as in the past 2 decades.[9] Poverty rates, defined as people living on a maximum of $1.90 per day, should have gone down to 104.1 million people by the end of 2020, but COVID-19 reversed this. The ADB report estimates the number of people living in poverty increased to 182.4 million by the end of 2020 using the $1.90 poverty line. Based on current GDP forecasts for a rebound in growth in 2021, the number of people living in extreme poverty in Developing Asia will decline to 132.5 million in 2021 and 104.4 million in 2022.

The United Nations *Sustainable Development Goals Report 2000* estimates that South Asia will be one of the most affected regions with an additional 32 million people living below the international poverty line due to COVID-19.[10] While these estimates may vary depending on the pace of recovery, they reveal the economic distress of the pandemic. Households in the affected sectors will suffer disproportionately. Poverty rates, for example, could double in Viet Nam for workers in manufacturing, dependent on imported inputs, and in some Pacific island countries where tourism is the largest employer.[11] Women are more likely than men to work in sectors requiring face-to-face interaction, such as tourism, retail, and hospitality. These sectors are the most affected by social distancing and mitigation measures and suffer a disproportionate impact from shutdowns due to COVID-19.

Governments have turned to the task of restoring long-term and sustainable economic growth. The initial reaction to COVID-19 centered on meeting immediate needs, like supporting medical first responders and ensuring that hospitals had necessary medicines, supplies, and equipment. The economic stimulus that followed aimed to achieve economic recovery through such measures as cash transfers, subsidies, and increased spending to support specific sectors. In 2021, there are signs that the Asia and Pacific region is reversing the impact of COVID-19 and resuming positive rates of economic growth. The Asian Infrastructure and Investment Bank studied a sample of 24 engineering, procurement, and contracting (EPC) companies across the region.[12]

---

5   74th Commission Session, United Nations Economic and Social Commission for Asia and the Pacific. 2018. *Inequality in Asia and the Pacific in the Era of the 2030 Agenda for Sustainable Development*. Bangkok: UNESCAP.

6   ADB. 2018. *Strategy 2030: Achieving a Prosperous, Inclusive, Resilient, and Sustainable Asia and the Pacific*. Manila.

7   United Nations Environment Programme. 2019. *Emissions Gap Report 2019*. Nairobi: UNEP.

8   UNESCAP. 2019. *Asia and the Pacific SDG Progress Report 2019*. UNESCAP: Bangkok.

9   ADB. 2021. *Asian Development Outlook 2021: Financing a Green and Inclusive Recovery*. April.

10   United Nations (UN). 2020. *UN Sustainable Development Goals Report, 2020*. New York: UN.

11   World Bank. 2020. *East Asia and Pacific in the Time of COVID-19*. Washington, DC.

12   The selected companies are mainly from Japan (6), the Republic of Korea (7), India (2), Turkey (2), the People's Republic of China (5), and Indonesia (2).

They found that despite devoting more resources to immediate COVID-19-related needs affecting project financing, completion, and future project development, the infrastructure sector nonetheless remained resilient in most Asian markets. EPC firms also showed signs of stock price recovery, strong revenues, and sound financials.[13]

COVID-19 may give the region a prime opportunity to not only catch up on environmental targets, but also lay the foundation and build back better for a green, inclusive, and resilient transition. A recent survey on emergency fiscal response shows that strong support for green investments within stimulus packages will accelerate the speed of economic impact. The survey of 231 officials from central banks, finance ministries, and economic experts from G20 countries looked at the relative performance of 25 fiscal recovery policy models across four categories: economic multiplier, climate impact, speed of implementation, and overall desirability.

The survey identified five models demonstrating the most impact on the economic multiplier and climate impact: energy retrofits, clean physical infrastructure, education and training, natural capital investment, and clean energy research and development.[14] Figure 3 shows which relief policy measures have the most impact on recovery according to the survey. Investments located in the center right of Figure 3 show good performance regarding implementation speed and the long-run multiplier. These policy measures include liquidity support for startups, small and medium households (D); support for basic needs (K); and direct cash transfers (O). Non-conditional airline bailouts did not appear in any of the experts' top 10 policy measures.

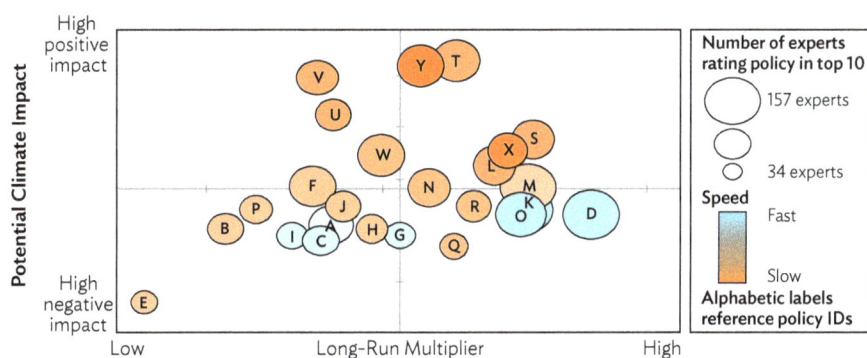

Figure 3: Results of Global Survey of Fiscal Recovery Policies

A	Temporary waiver of interest payments
B	Assisted bankruptcy (super Chapter 11)
C	Liquidity support for large corporations
D	Liquidity support for households, start-ups and SMEs
E	Airline bailouts
F	Not for profits, education, research, health inst. bailouts
G	Reduction in VAT and other goods and services taxes
H	Income tax cuts
I	Business tax deferrals
J	Business tax relief for strategic and structural adj.
K	Direct provision of basic needs
L	Education investment
M	Healthcare investment
N	Worker retaining
O	Targeted direct cash transfers or temporary wage increases
P	Rural support policies
Q	Traditional transport infrastructure investment
R	Project-based local infrastructure grants
S	Connectivity infrastructure investment
T	Clean energy infrastructure investment
U	Building upgrades (energy efficient)
V	Green spaces and natural infrastructure investment
W	Disaster preparedness, capacity building
X	General R&D spending
Y	Clean R&D spending

ID = identification, R&D = research and development, SMEs = small and medium-sized enterprises, VAT = value-added tax.

Source: C. Hepburn et al. 2020. Will COVID-19 Fiscal Recovery Packages Accelerate Or Retard Progress On Climate Change? *Oxford Review of Economic Policy.* 36(S1).

[13] See https://www.aiib.org/en/news-events/media-center/blog/2020/Impact-of-COVID-19-on-the-EPC-Sector-in-Asia-Out look-Remains-Robust-for-the-Infrastructure-Sector.html.

[14] C. Hepburn et al. Will COVID-19 Fiscal Recovery Packages Accelerate Or Retard Progress On Climate Change? *Oxford Review of Economic Policy.* 36(S1).

The challenge after COVID-19 lies in having the resources to increase green investment and sustain it at higher levels, including adaptation and resilience against pressing fiscal and financing constraints. This requires effective domestic resource mobilization for infrastructure and basic services, as well as sustainable development finance and poverty alleviation. Building back better requires policies, institutions, and skills to build social resiliency, and resource mobilization and economic growth policies to support social and productive infrastructure and technology development. It will also require policy changes to ensure the correct market signals, supporting policies to sustain "green investments" such as subsidy reform/subsidy swaps and import duties on certain equipment, and carbon taxes/pricing over the longer term. The Republic of Korea, during the global financial crisis of 2008–2009, put in place one of the most successful green stimulus packages, with around 80% of spending on green investments. Unfortunately, only a handful of economies followed this example. Only around 16% of total global stimulus spending from 2008–2009 was green.[15]

To meet the large financing requirements for sustainable infrastructure, countries have to strengthen their capacity to raise resources from all sources, including at the national and subnational level.[16] Financial flows from domestic resources and the private sector will provide most of the financing, supported by funding from international institutions to close the infrastructure financing gap. Meeting the large needs for sustainable infrastructure requires resolute efforts to mobilize additional resources through tax and expenditure policies and will be especially important at the subnational level. Of the $26 trillion estimated by ADB for sustainable infrastructure investment from 2016 to 2030, a significant proportion will be related to urban areas.[17] Local governments have to increase domestic revenues to strengthen fiscal capacities at local levels, which are typically low in developing economies. COVID-19 worsened the situation at all levels of government due to increased pressure on expenditures and decreased tax revenues (Box 1). In response to the need to mobillize more domestic resources, ADB has established a regional hub to improve domestic resource mobilization and international tax cooperation that will promote operational support, knowledge sharing and institutional capacity development across the Asia and Pacific region.[18]

DMCs are often unable to attract sufficient long-term private financing for infrastructure investments despite abundant global savings and historically low long-term interest rates. Increasing access to and reducing the cost of private capital requires action on several fronts. Deepening domestic capital market development can help mobilize private finance through public policy to address underlying market, policy, and governance failures. Countries should also consider guarantees and credit enhancements offered by international financial institutions.

Investors have recognized the importance of promoting infrastructure as an asset class to increase access to private savings. This calls for developing a pipeline of bankable and fiscally sustainable projects, standardizing project contracts where possible, ensuring transparency and information disclosure for investors and other stakeholders, and establishing sound regulatory and institutional frameworks, all of which are vital in promoting infrastructure as an asset class. Contractual standardization in the bidding stage is critical in reducing cost and complexity and providing comparability. In terms of the regulatory framework, ensuring the development of

---

[15] Barbier, E. 2010. Green Stimulus is Not Sufficient for a Global Green Recovery. *VoxEU*. 3 Jun.

[16] ADB Office of Public–Private Partnerships Thematic Group Secretariat (OPPP-TGS) is supporting subnational entities under Technical Assistance (54036-001) on Creating Investable Cities in a Post-COVID-19 Asia and the Pacific—Enhancing Competitiveness and Resilience through Quality Infrastructure. This TA emphasizes development of standardized frameworks and capacity building at the subnational level to improve the quality of the pipeline of municipal projects by (i) supporting early-stage project preparation; (ii) unlocking own sources of revenue to support infrastructure development; and (iii) raising more capital from the private sector, including through public–private partnerships.

[17] ADB. 2017. *Meeting Asia's Infrastructure Needs*. Manila.

[18] See ADB. 2020. ADB to Establish Regional Hub to Help Economies Improve Domestic Resource Mobilization and Tax Cooperation. News release. 17 September.

BOX 1	**Asia and the Pacific: Progress in Mobilizing Domestic Revenues Set Back by COVID-19**

The Organisation for Economic Co-operation and Development (OECD) report *Revenue Statistics in Asian and Pacific Economies* (2020) highlights the progress made across the region to improve tax-to-gross domestic product (GDP) ratios and domestic resource mobilization in 2018. However, tax revenues in 2020 decreased because of the coronavirus disease (COVID-19). In 2018, more than two-thirds of the 21 countries in Asia and the Pacific—including Bhutan, Mongolia, Nauru, and the People's Republic of China for the first time—showed rising tax-to-GDP levels. Overall, the region has maintained a healthy growth in tax yields in line with GDP growth rates over the past 5 years. There is also significant variation in tax-to-GDP ratios from 11.9% in Indonesia to 35.4% in Nauru, which was the only country exceeding the OECD tax-to-GDP average ratio of 34.3%. Eight of the 11 Asian countries had a tax-to-GDP ratio under 20% and 7 of the 10 Pacific economies showed a tax-to-GDP ratio over 23%. The report also estimated that that tax and non-tax revenues will decline because of the pandemic. Countries' tax administrations are impacted in different ways depending on economic structure; those relying on taxes from natural resources, tourism, and trade are the most exposed. The report notes that environment and climate-oriented taxes do not have a large role but could help boost revenues in a green recovery from the pandemic.

Source: OECD. 2020. *Revenue Statistics in Asian and Pacific Economies 2020.* Paris: OECD Publishing. https://doi.org/10.1787/d47d0ae3-enOECD.

domestic capital markets also supports infrastructure as an asset class, especially in DMCs that can reduce currency mismatch through local currency financing.[19]

COVID-19 revealed the volatility of capital flows and the limits of conventional monetary policies. A recent working paper by the IMF shows that risks to macroeconomic and financial stability caused by volatile capital flows are often problematic in addressing traditional monetary policy tools.[20] Central banks often face a difficult tradeoff in responding to external shocks like COVID-19 that cause sharp exchange rate depreciations and capital outflows. If inflation expectations are poorly anchored and tend to be off-target, central banks are forced to choose between sharply raising interest rates to keep inflation stable—at the cost of a steep output decline—and pursuing a more passive policy that risks allowing inflation to become unmoored. The model suggests that foreign exchange intervention and capital controls can improve policy tradeoffs considerably under certain conditions, especially for economies that have less well-anchored inflation expectations and are more vulnerable to shocks causing capital outflow and exchange rate pressures. However, governments need more innovative approaches to expand access to capital for infrastructure investment.

New and transformative financial instruments like green bonds and land value capture to promote transit-oriented development in urban settings can help expand the choice of investment options and risk profiles, even with the challenge of developing financial instruments for municipal-level and small-scale infrastructure. Social impact investors would be a source of finance particularly for projects with a double bottom line combining moderate returns with social and economic impact for the poor. This could include bundling

---

[19] OECD. 2018. *Roadmap to Infrastructure as an Asset Class, Argentina Presidency.* Paris: OECD.
[20] Suman S. Basu et al. 2020. A Conceptual Model for the Integrated Policy Framework. *IMF Working Papers.* Washington, DC: IMF.

small projects to reduce costs and achieve scale. A diversification of financial instruments has the potential to de-risk infrastructure assets. ADB and other multilateral development banks have innovative credit enhancement instruments to allocate project risk to catalyze private investment. Other financial instruments offered by multilateral development banks, such as blended finance, can also help to draw in private funding and offer risk mitigation. Support for local currency capital market development, supported by myriad development finance instruments (e.g., grants, loans), can help DMCs mobilize investment resources by expanding the tax base and developing local bond markets.

The greening of the financial system can have a profound impact across the economy and help ensure macro-level stability, but the frequency and severity of extreme weather events can threaten infrastructure assets. The G20 requested the Financial Stability Board (FSB) to study the impact of climate change on financial stability. In July 2020, the FSB released a report on financial authorities' experience in assessing climate-related risks in monitoring financial stability. The report surveyed FSB members, international organizations, and the private sector, and found variations in how climate-related risks are viewed.

Around three-quarters of respondents had plans to assess climate-related risks and incorporate these assessments in their financial stability monitoring efforts. Most focused on how the impact of climate change caused variations in asset prices and credit quality. A minority of the financial institutions surveyed also looked at the effects on operational, legal, and liability risks. Investors adopted standardized frameworks to account for the impacts of climate change on their investments. For example, the Task Force on Climate-related Financial Disclosures—established by the G20 to represent private sector organizations with capitalizations of nearly $12 trillion—promotes greater transparency and consistency in accounting for and reporting climate opportunities and risks.[21]

---

[21] Financial Stability Board (FSB). 2020. Report on FSB Members' Work on Financial Stability Implications of Climate Risks.

SECTION

2

PUBLIC INVESTMENT EFFICIENCY IN INFRASTRUCTURE

Although infrastructure investment has been useful in stimulating growth, the impact of COVID-19 will reduce capacity to fund infrastructure from government budgets due to lower revenues. COVID-19 may give the region a prime opportunity not only to catch up on environmental targets, but also to lay the foundation and build back better for a green, inclusive, and resilient transition. To meet the large financing requirements for sustainable infrastructure, countries have to strengthen their capacity to raise resources from all sources, including at the national and subnational level. Financial flows from domestic resources and the private sector will provide most of the financing, supported by funding from international institutions to close the infrastructure financing gap.

Economist John Maynard Keynes argued for public investment to support countercyclical fiscal policy, providing a justification for public works programs that restore economic growth and employment. Investment in public infrastructure (e.g., water and sewage, highways and roads, airports, and mass transit) contributed to higher United States (US) productivity, suggesting that the reduction in productivity between 1970 to 1980 might have been due to lower infrastructure investment. Indeed, every dollar invested in the interstate highway network from 1954 to 2001 in the United States added $6 of economic productivity and growth.[22]

The multiplier due to public investment is clear though its impact will vary by sector. The result the US achieved in this time may be higher than what can be expected in a developing country today due to the pandemic. The pandemic impact is different because it is not just a demand shock—it is both a supply and a demand shock. The large impact in the US was also due in part to its advanced-economy status with unprecedented economic growth during that time. Conversely, the infrastructure gaps in the US in the 1950s–1960s was less than what many DMCs in Asia now face, suggesting that the multiplier effects in Asia could be greater.

---

22 Jean-Paul Rodriguez. 2009. *The Geography of Transport Systems*. New York: Routledge.

Synchronized global infrastructure investment can help restore growth, reduce scarring, and promote climate goals. If countries act concurrently, public infrastructure investment can restore growth both domestically and globally by means of trade linkages. This positive economic "spillover" impact can result in an additional boost to world output. The spillovers resulting from increased demand have greater effect if growth is weak and interest rates are low. According to the IMF, if advanced economies with fiscal space increase infrastructure investment spending to 0.5% of GDP in 2021, raise spending to 1.0% of GDP in 2022, maintaining spending at that level until 2025, and if countries with limited fiscal space spend around one-third of that amount during the same period, global growth could increase around 2.0%. If countries were to implement spending on their own and not simultaneously, the addition to global GDP would be under 1.2% of GDP (Figure 4). In emerging markets, positive public investment shocks increase output in both the short and medium terms. Public investment of one percentage point of GDP can increase output by about 0.2% in the same year and 0.5% 4 years after the investment, provided the investment is in projects that result in positive social and economic returns. The effects of public investment on output are more short-lived in low-income developing countries.[23]

Figure 4: Impact of Global Push for Infrastructure Investment

A synchronized approach
Global GDP could rise by nearly 2% if countries simulataneously invested in high-quality infrastructure improvements
(percent deviation from baseline)

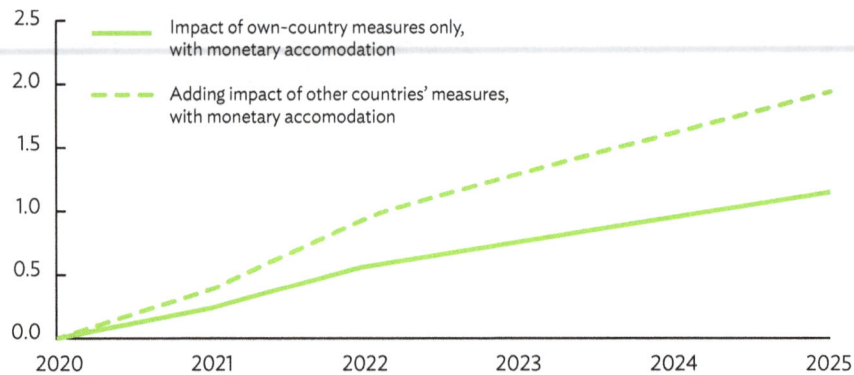

GDP = gross domestic product.

Source: IMF. 2020. *G20 Surveillance Note*. November.

There is a significant need to combine infrastructure stimulus with a plan to improve the capacity and capability of the institutions managing and investing in public infrastructure assets. In the short-term, the Global Infrastructure Hub (GIH) found the impact of investment on the macroeconomy least likely to be affected by the size and labor intensity of construction activity. This made infrastructure a go-to form of stimulus in previous downturns for "shovel-ready" or maintenance projects that are quickly launched. However, if assets are unproductive, the overall impact on output will be lower.

The GIH study suggests that public institutions that can manage the nature and quality of the investment have a positive impact on infrastructure assets' long-term viability. Investing early, even during recessions, together with

---

[23] IMF. 2020. *Well Spent: How Infrastructure Governance Can End Waste in Public Investment.* Washington, DC.

increased fiscal spending, provides critical opportunities to promote sustainable growth across infrastructure sectors. Authorities need to look at the investments on a portfolio basis and the systematic resilience and long-term net-zero impact of investments when determining which infrastructure investments to make. In COVID-19 recovery, governments need to invest quickly in "shovel-ready" projects, but these need to contribute to long-term and sustainable vision.

The World Bank has reviewed evidence of fiscal adjustments implemented in several countries in the 1990s and found that cutbacks in public investment were associated with a decline in economic growth. Instead of resulting in greater fiscal sustainability, cutting public investment could result in a reduction of economic growth that did not support fiscal solvency. If the efficiency of the public investment was relatively low resulting in poor selection of projects and weak project implementation, and the investment was not transformed into productive public capital stock, the public investment resulted in more limited long-term output gains.[24]

The impact of public investment on economic growth will likely not be realized or may be negative if the capacity to manage public investment is low or resources are wasted due to corruption. Efficient public sector investment management depends on the quality of allocative efficiency; that is, resources are allocated to projects generating the optimum positive rate of economic or social return. However, this rate of return very much depends on how effectively the public investments are managed—from planning and budgeting, to operation and maintenance (O&M) of the public asset. There are caveats to realizing the benefits of infrastructure investment. These are based on a sustainable fiscal position, manageable debt, and limiting new borrowing to investment projects yielding suitable social and economic returns. The achievement of fiscal and external debt sustainability should be anchored in a transparent and strong public investment management system.

The enabling environment for project preparation is a key driver for quality investments and outcomes. Many factors determine the quality of the enabling environment, including economic, regulatory, and legal frameworks and institutional and governance capabilities. The enabling environment requires a near state-of-the-art professional capacity in procurement, financial management, audit, engineering, and law. In 2020, the GIH-produced InfraCompass, which ranks the infrastructure enabling environment globally, found much variation in the quality of regulatory frameworks, including the need to improve PPP frameworks. It noted that governments need to implement reforms to improve governance, the implementation of regulatory frameworks, and the stability and sustainability of fiscal management.

The regulatory quality, credit ratings, and rule of law show the biggest performance gaps, with advanced economies ranking higher than low and middle-income countries. Singapore ranks number one in governance; however, the Asia and Pacific region on average underperforms on infrastructure governance when compared to Europe. This measurement refers to institutions that can support the rule of law and having transparent, effective, and independent decision-making procedures for project planning and preparation, resource allocation , and project implementation. On a scale of 0–100, Asia and the Pacific scores 55 on governance of infrastructure compared to 70 for Europe.[25] In effect, infrastructure governance is a "missing middle" between the policy and regulatory environment and the structuring and transaction phase of infrastructure investments. The missing middle is instrumental in ensuring quality outcomes and stimulating economic growth post COVID-19.

---

24 Frank, J. et al. 2014. *The Power of Public Investment Management: Transforming Resources into Assets for Growth. Directions in Development.* Washington, DC: World Bank.

25 Global Infrastructure Hub, InfraCompass 2020. InfraCompass objectively quantifies the strength of the infrastructure enabling environment by aggregating data for 81 countries. InfraCompass ranks countries across eight drivers: governance, regulatory frameworks, permits, planning, procurement, activity, funding capacity, and financial markets.

PUBLIC INVESTMENT MANAGEMENT— DRIVER FOR RESTORING SUSTAINABLE ECONOMIC GROWTH

Governments need to identify gaps in infrastructure governance pertaining to planning, managing, and implementing public investments to improve the quality of infrastructure project pipelines. Although there is great variation among countries and levels of government in terms of the quality of infrastructure governance, there is scope to improve infrastructure governance by linking medium-term fiscal and budget frameworks to infrastructure planning, inter-agency coordination including between national and subnational levels, and improving the rigor of investment selection, appraisal and risk analysis, and management of projects.

The IMF uses Public Investment Management Assessments (PIMAs) to assess infrastructure governance for the full project investment cycle.[26] The PIMA reviews and analyzes the efficiency of infrastructure investment, defined as the ratio of the capital stock of infrastructure investment per capita to indicators measuring the quality of and access to infrastructure. It examines trends in productivity, infrastructure quality, growth, and public investment, providing an analysis based on a cross-country index of public investment efficiency and the application of the PIMA tool across a range of country income levels.

Average public investment efficiency varies widely across and within regions, from an efficiency gap of about 21% in Europe to 48% in sub-Saharan Africa. Efficiency gap estimates provide a measure of wasted resources and hint at potential institutional weaknesses. ADB joined IMF missions to conduct several PIMAs in ADB DMCs. Figure 5 shows the public efficiency investment score on public infrastructure investment across regions.[27]

---

26 IMF. 2018. *Public Investment Management Review and Update*. Washington, DC.
27 IMF. 2020. *Well Spent: How Infrastructure Governance Can End Waste in Public Investment*. Washington, DC.

Figure 5: Public Investment Efficiency Score by Region

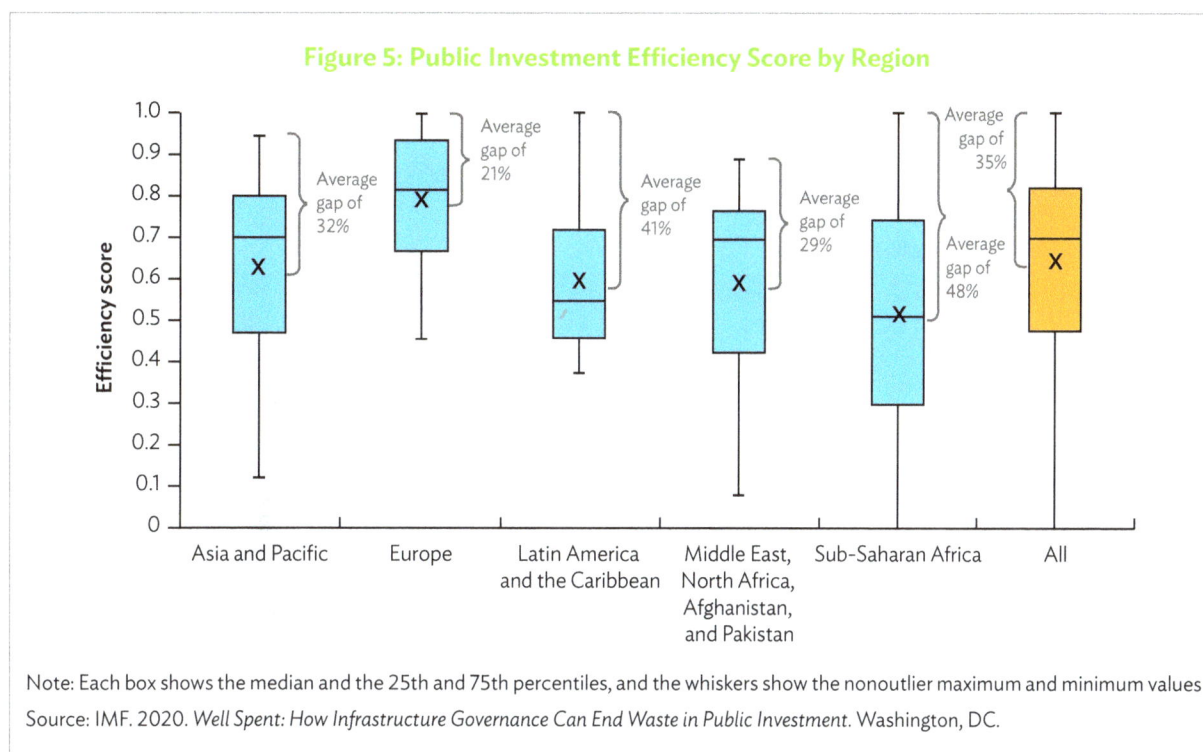

Note: Each box shows the median and the 25th and 75th percentiles, and the whiskers show the nonoutlier maximum and minimum values
Source: IMF. 2020. *Well Spent: How Infrastructure Governance Can End Waste in Public Investment.* Washington, DC.

PIMAs assess institutions from three perspectives: institutional design, effectiveness, and reform priority. They evaluate 15 of the main institutions responsible for planning, allocating, and implementing public investment. These public investment management (PIM) institutions are part of a broader group of institutions responsible for public financial management. Institutional design assesses investment institutions (public investment rules, legal and regulatory procedures, and standardized roles) based on "good international practices." Effectiveness assesses the practical implementation of public investment laws, instruments, and legal and regulatory policies. Reform priorities identify and recommend policies or procedures that address shortcomings and strengthen infrastructure governance.

Emerging markets show overall better design scores than low-income and developing countries (LIDCs). Figure 6 shows the global quality of the design of policies for key elements of public investment management. Emerging markets have better overall scores for the design of policies than low-income countries (footnote 26). It is interesting to note that national and sector planning for low-income countries and advanced economies is similar, possibly because planning is a historical legacy of donor technical assistance in many LIDCs. Emerging markets have relatively better-designed PIM policies for availability of funding and company regulation, while both emerging markets and LIDCs show similar weaknesses in project appraisal and selection and management of PPPs.

Countries are better at designing PIM institutions than managing them effectively. Almost all countries showed higher PIMA scores for all PIM institutions on design than on effectiveness. While many countries have formal national sector plans, these are seldom properly costed, aligned with the medium-term framework and annual budget, or used to inform public investment decisions. Though most countries have procedures to ensure transparent procurement, PIMAs showed significant noncompliance. Similarly, even monitoring project implementation rarely results in corrective actions. While some countries have standardized technical criteria for project selection following good international practices, governments often do not implement them (footnote 26).

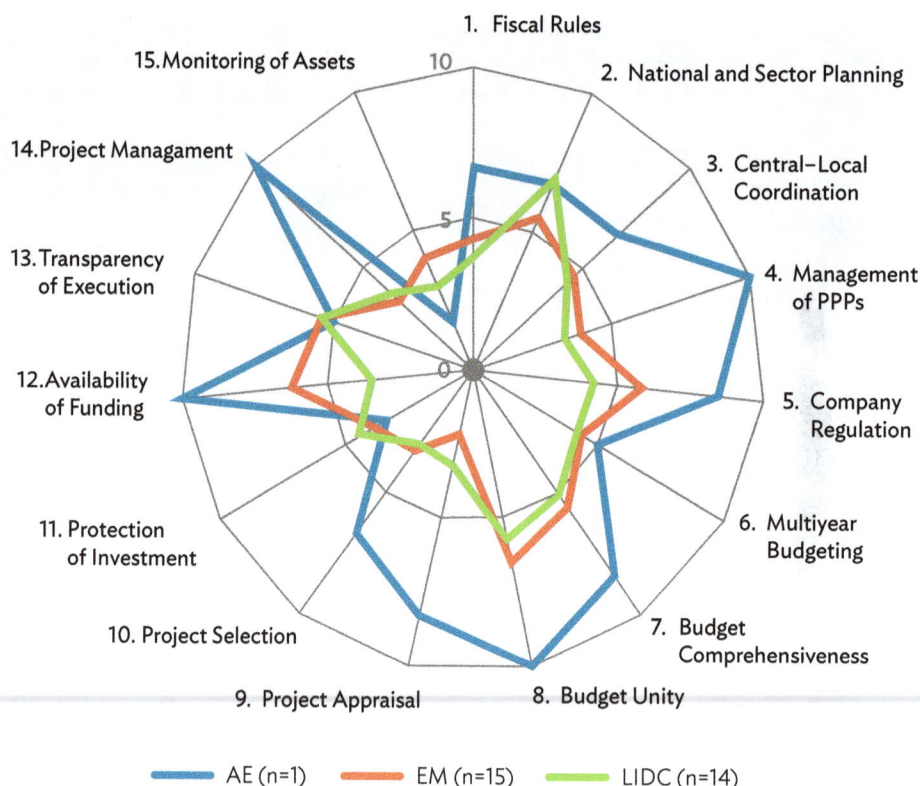

Figure 6: Ranking of Public Investment Management Institutions by Scores in Design

1. Fiscal Rules
2. National and Sector Planning
3. Central–Local Coordination
4. Management of PPPs
5. Company Regulation
6. Multiyear Budgeting
7. Budget Comprehensiveness
8. Budget Unity
9. Project Appraisal
10. Project Selection
11. Protection of Investment
12. Availability of Funding
13. Transparency of Execution
14. Project Managament
15. Monitoring of Assets

AE (n=1)   EM (n=15)   LIDC (n=14)

AE = advanced economy, EM = emerging market, LIDC = low-income and developing country, PPP = public–private partnership.
Source: IMF. 2018. *Public Investment Management–Review and Update*. Washington, DC.

To strengthen PIM institutions, emerging markets should adopt and improve processes for screening, selecting, appraising, and approving investment projects. Countries will also benefit from better supervision of public infrastructure and PPPs and linking strategic planning with capital budgeting. Also, there are considerable economic dividends if efficiency gaps are minimized; the most efficient public sector investments can generate twice the growth of public investment expenditure compared to the least efficient. PIMAs identify significant areas where institutions shaping the planning, allocation, and implementation of public investments must be strengthened. Governments can reduce up to two-thirds of public investment inefficiencies by strengthening PIM institutions. Figure 7 shows the difference in growth rates among six Asian countries based on either no change in efficiency or closing the efficiency gap over 5 years. The improvement in the projected growth rate based on closing the efficiency gap ranges from 1.9% to 4.78% of GDP.

Figure 7: Improving Public Investment Efficiency Could Increase Growth as Percent of Gross Domestic Product

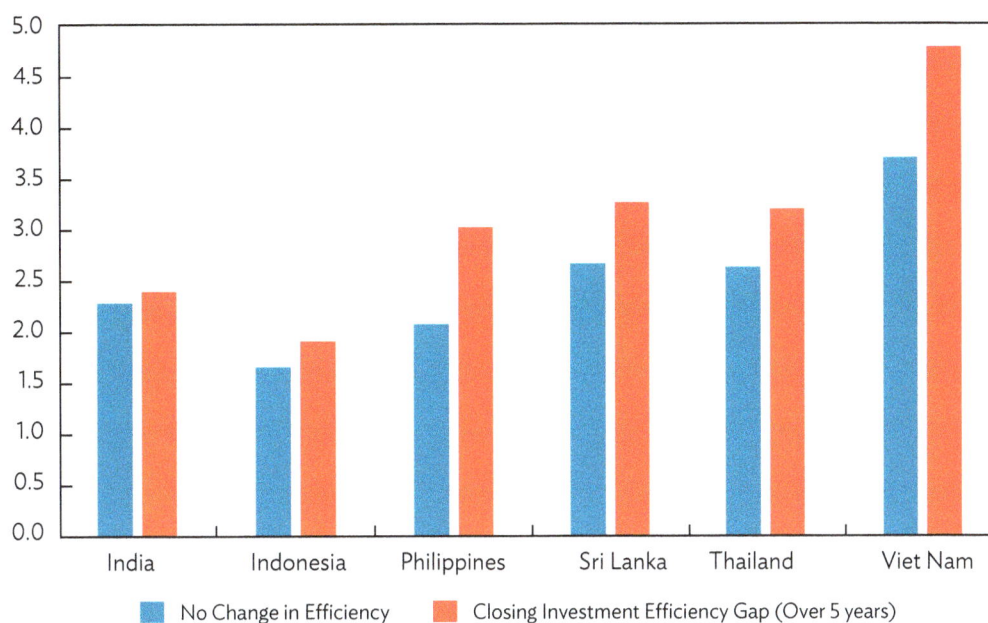

Source: H. Vu, O. Bizimana, and M. Nozaki. 2020. Boosting Infrastructure in Emerging Asia. In G. Schwartz, M. Fouad, T. Hansen, and G. Verdier, eds. 2020. *Well Spent: How Strong Infrastructure Governance Can End Waste in Public Investment.* Washington, DC: IMF.

The PIMA reviews find on average that countries fail to realize 30% of the economic benefits of infrastructure investments because of inefficiencies in the investment process (footnote 26). The range of lost potential benefits, however, ranges from 30% to 50% of the investment amount (Figure 8). The gap in efficiency is particularly acute in lower-income countries as they tend to have weaker institutional capacity related to funding, management, and project monitoring. On the other hand, emerging markets show progress in integrating efficiencies into their PIM institutions. PIM institutions in emerging markets tend to be strongest in Europe, weakest in the Middle East and Central Asia, and more variable in the Asia and Pacific region.

Figure 8: Public Sector Investment Efficiency Varies by Income Levels

Road to nowhere
Countries waste anywhere from 30% up to 50% of the money they spend on infrastructure
(percentage deviation from full efficiency)

EFFICIENCY LOSS

Low Income Developing Countries	53%
Emerging Market Economies	34%
Advanced Economies	15%

Source: G. Schwartz, M. Fouad, T. Hansen, and G. Verdier. 2020. *Well Spent, How Strong Infrastructure Governance Can End Waste in Public Investment.*

Governance and institutional capacity gained greater significance in crisis management, with capable and resilient public sector institutions that can ensure accountability, inclusiveness, rule of law, transparency, and reduced corruption remaining critical. An ADB working paper analyzed the interaction between governance and development outcomes across various dimensions using the Worldwide Governance Indicators (WGI).[28] The paper shows government effectiveness as the most important factor in the quality of civil service, capacity development, and effective policy design and implementation. The analysis confirms, however, that the sensitivity of GDP growth to governance is lower in developing Asia than in other regions.

This "Asian conundrum" may be due to widely divergent governance indicators within Asia's five subregions. An important finding of this analysis is that good governance is linked to GDP per capita and to wider development outcomes including the Human Development Index, poverty headcount ratio, gender inequality ratio, under-5 mortality ratio, years of schooling under 15, and quality infrastructure supply. The analysis results hold for a composite governance index comprising an unweighted average across all six WGIs. Developing Asia ranks the highest among developing regions of the world across the WGIs but is below the average for the OECD (Figure 9).

---

[28] A. Baluga. and B. Carrasco, 2020. The Role of Geography in Shaping Governance Performance. *ADB Sustainable Development Working Paper Series*. No. 73. December. Manila. The Worldwide Governance Indicators (WGI) is an index developed by the World Bank to measure overall governance in public institutions. The WGI framework includes following indicators: (i) voice and accountability, (ii) political stability and absence of violence, (iii) government effectiveness, (iv) regulatory quality, (v) rule of law, and (vi) control of corruption.

Figure 9: Worldwide Governance Indicator Regional Comparison (Estimates, 2018)

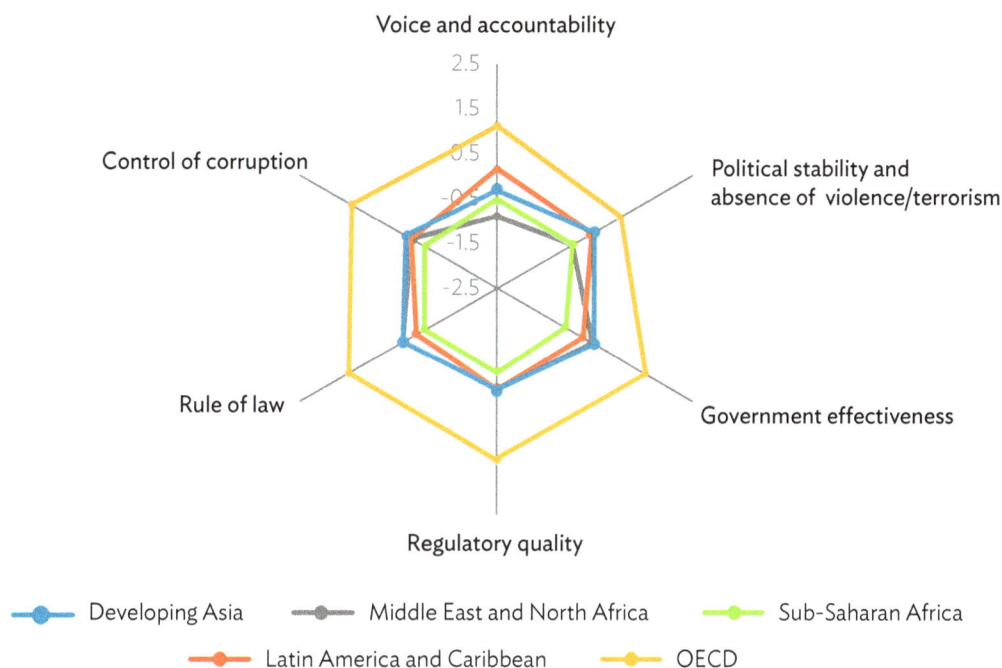

OECD = Organisation for Economic Co-operation and Development.

Source: ADB graph from World Governance Indicator database (accessed October 2020). (World Bank) http://info.worldbank.org/governance/wg.

Public sector investment, including investment by government entities and SOEs, is the principal source of infrastructure investment in developing and emerging market economies. Figure 10 shows that public investment accounts for 83% of infrastructure investment globally. Of this, 66% is from SOEs and 34% is from public agency investments. In comparison, 17% is from the private sector in the form of PPPs. SOEs accounted for 74% of total infrastructure investment in East Asia and the Pacific, of which 84% is from the PRC (60%) and Indonesia (24%). In South Asia, SOEs contributed 44% of total infrastructure investment. Globally, public banks and direct government investment financed 75% of all project commitments in DMCs.[29]

---

[29] World Bank, PPIAF. 2019. Who Sponsors Infrastructure Projects? Disentangling Public and Private Contributions. This report documents and analyzes the SOE/public project data collected and compares it to the Private Participation in Infrastructure database, to see the relative proportion of investment commitments made by the public, SOEs, and the private sector to infrastructure projects at the global, regional, and sector levels in 2017.

Figure 10: Public and Private Investment and State-owned Enterprises

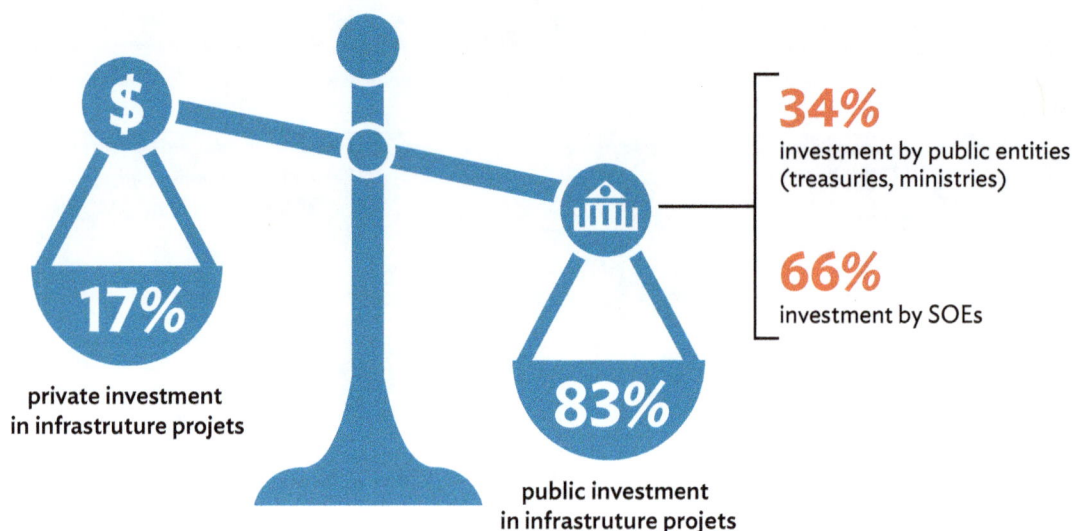

34%
investment by public entities
(treasuries, ministries)

66%
investment by SOEs

17%
private investment
in infrastruture projets

83%
public investment
in infrastruture projets

SOE = state-owned enterprise.
Source: World Bank, PPIAF. 2019. *Who Sponsors Infrastructure Projects? Disentangling Public and Private Contributions.* Washington, DC.

Many governments adopt reforms to help SOEs fulfill their public mandates and perform efficiently. The IMF compared the financial performance of about one million individual SOEs across 109 countries to private firms. The database includes firms that mostly represent advanced and emerging market economies and a smaller group from low-income countries.[30] Figure 11 shows that labor productivity and profits are lower in SOEs in comparison with those of private firms. Regional and country studies for the PRC, the Russian Federation, and in central, eastern, and southeastern Europe also find lower labor productivity and profits in SOEs.

The IMF comparison suggests this difference could reflect the cost of providing services at below-market prices for delivering services to poor communities or promoting employment in accordance with government policies, but other factors may be at play, like less efficient SOEs. If the differences are due to less efficient SOEs, economic productivity can decrease. ADB published a guidance note on SOE reform in sovereign projects and programs. This publication identified challenges for SOE reforms. The challenges are manifested in a variety of areas including diffuse and weak accountability, multiple mandates, unlevel playing field with the private sector in terms of subsidies and preferential treatment, and poor governance related to requirements for disclosure and transparency.[31]

---

[30] IMF. 2020. Policies to Support People During the COVID-19 Pandemic, State-Owned Enterprises: The Other Government in IMF Fiscal Monitor, April 2020, Chapter 3. "Of the 969,000 firms in the sample, about 949,000 are fully private, 15,000 are majority state owned, and 4,000 are minority state owned. The database includes mainly firms from advanced and emerging market economies, with a smaller sample from low-income countries. The analysis uses SOE financial data, given that it is available for a large set of firms. For example, labor productivity is proxied by sales per employee, which does not necessarily reflect only the differences in technical efficiency. If SOEs are restricted to charging lower prices relative to private firms, this would have a negative effect on sales per employee."

[31] ADB. 2020. *Guidance Note on State-Owned-Enterprise Reform in Sovereign Projects and Programs.* February.

Figure 11: Performance of State-owned Enterprises Relative to Private Firms

1. Profits and Costs
(Percent)

2. Productivity
($ million per employee)

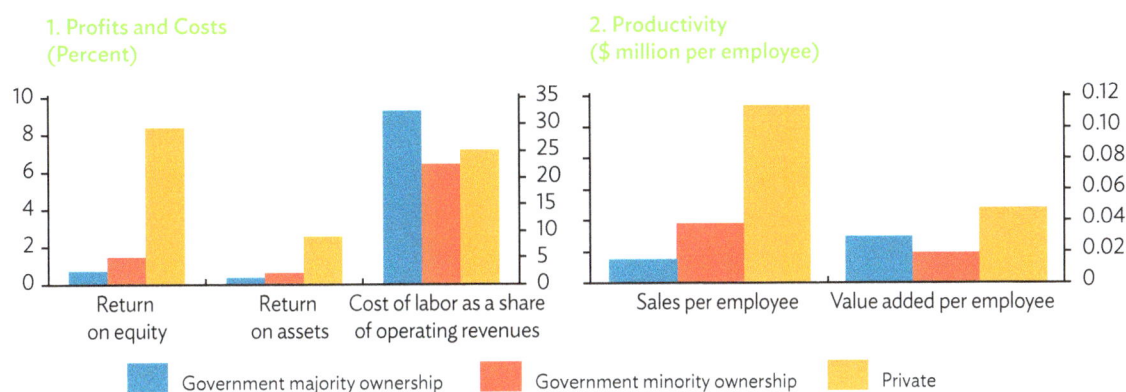

■ Government majority ownership   ■ Government minority ownership   ■ Private

Source: IMF. 2020. Policies to Support People During the COVID-19 Pandemic, State-Owned Enterprises: The Other Government in IMF Fiscal Monitor, April.

The sheer scope of infrastructure investment needed in DMC markets has led countries to seek more private investment to supplement the core role of public investment. The available investment capital from institutional investors has largely remained invested in developed markets due to perceived risks in the bankability and affordability of DMC infrastructure projects. The lack of global private investment in low-income countries is due in part to the need for efficient public investment and stronger institutional capacity to plan and deliver a pipeline of quality infrastructure projects.

The World Bank estimates that PPP investments by institutional investors such as pension funds and sovereign wealth funds into emerging markets and developing countries accounted for only 0.67% of total PPP investment or $1.9 billion from 2011 to the first half of 2017. Among the causes are lack of bankable projects, currency risks, rule of law, and fiscal and affordability risks among DMCs.[32] An ADB blog post emphasized that the lack of infrastructure investment has been further hampered by the impact of COVID-19, which led to some PPP projects being renegotiated, force majeure, and delays in construction.[33]

Efficient spending will be essential for fiscal management in a post-pandemic world to help countries grapple with limited fiscal space and increasing debt. Over the past decade, DMCs experienced the fastest increase in debt in over 50 years. Since 2010, total debt among developing countries increased by 60% of GDP to a peak of more than 170% of GDP in 2019. Without the PRC, debt went up by 20% of GDP, to 108%.[34] According to the World Bank, on average, debt-to-GDP ratios since 2010 have risen around 7% per year—almost three times faster than in the Latin American debt crisis of the 1970s. This increase, affecting all regions of the world, includes government and private debt. Though the existence of historically low interest rates mitigates the current risk of

---

32 The Public–Private Infrastructure Advisory Facility (PPIAF). 2020. Contribution of Institutional Investors: Private Investment in Infrastructure, 2011–2017. Washington, DC: World Bank Group.

33 ADB. 2020. Another COVID-19 Challenge: Saving Asia's Crucial Infrastructure Deals. Asian Development Blog. https://blogs.adb.org/another-covid-19-challenge-saving-asia-s-crucial-infrastructure-deals.

34 M.A. Kose et al. 2020. Caught by a Cresting Debt Wave; ibid Global Waves of Debt: Causes and Consequences in Finance & Development. Volume 57. Washington, DC: World Bank.

a global debt crisis, the pandemic can increase the risk that this debt will become a crisis as governments increase spending to provide social protection against COVID-19 while facing a reduced growth forecast per year from 2019 to 2024 (Figures 12 and 13). To offset this potential risk, the World Bank recommends that debt be spent on finance investments generating jobs and growth, stressing the need for greater transparency in the management and composition of this debt.[35]

Figure 12: Real Growth by Forecast Year, 2019–2024

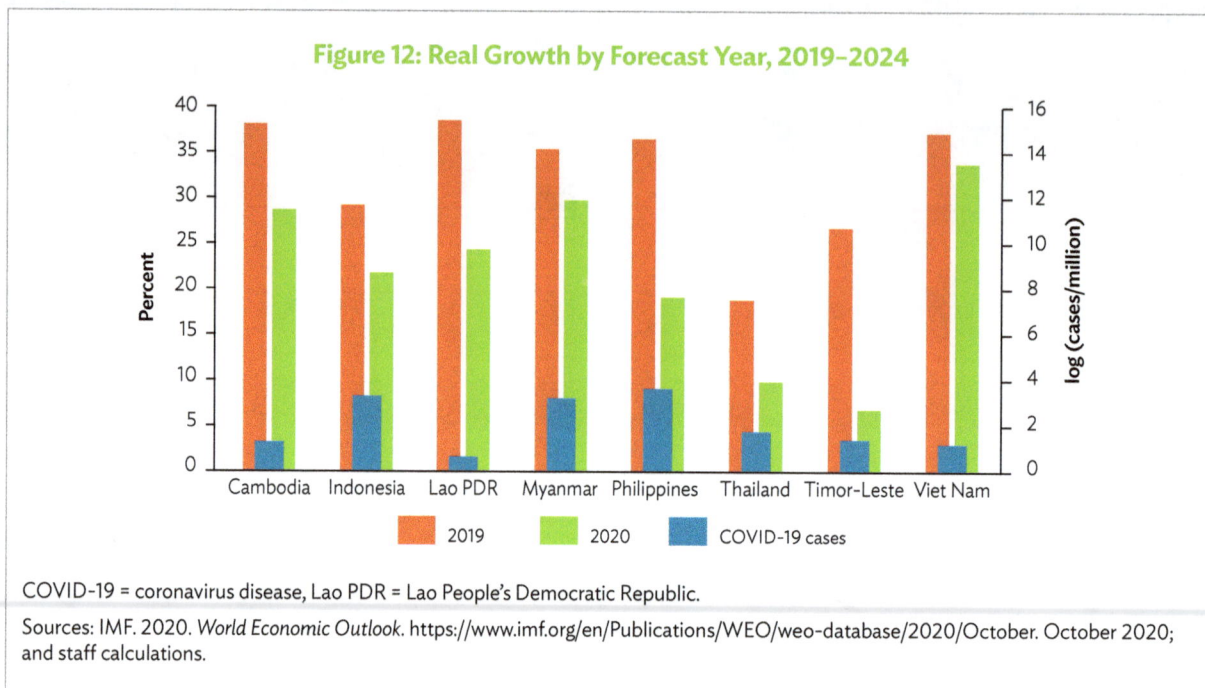

COVID-19 = coronavirus disease, Lao PDR = Lao People's Democratic Republic.

Sources: IMF. 2020. *World Economic Outlook*. https://www.imf.org/en/Publications/WEO/weo-database/2020/October. October 2020; and staff calculations.

Figure 13: Debt–Gross Domestic Product Ratio by Forecast Year, 2019–2024

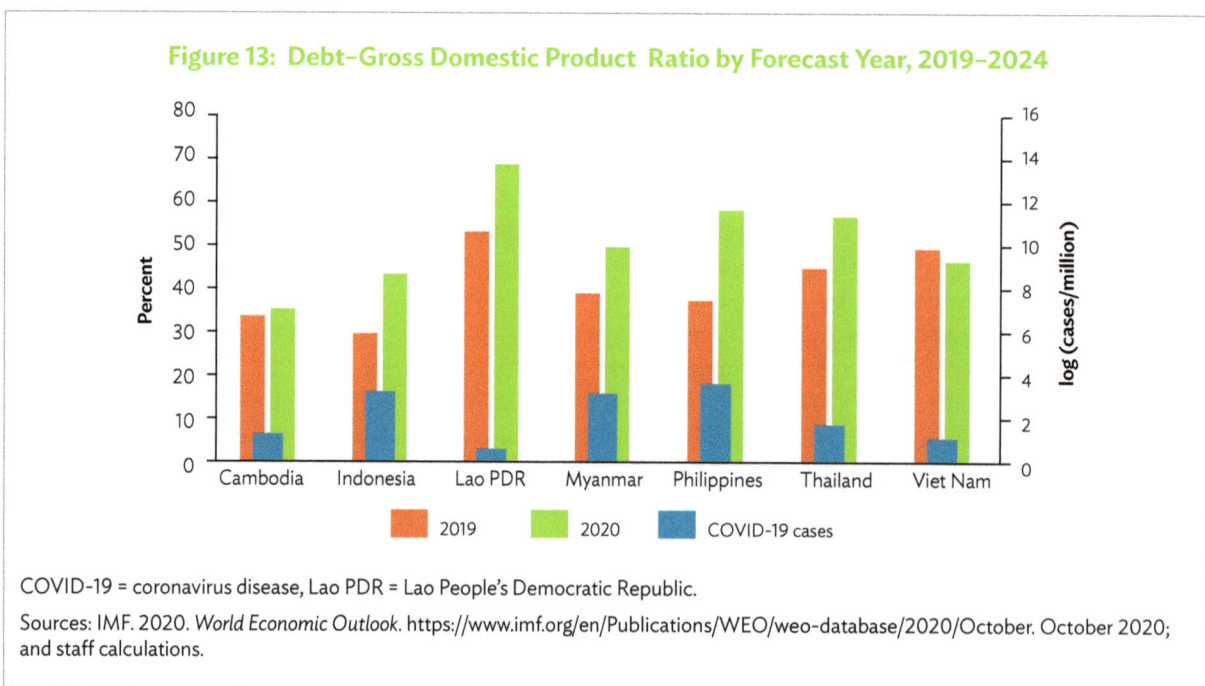

COVID-19 = coronavirus disease, Lao PDR = Lao People's Democratic Republic.

Sources: IMF. 2020. *World Economic Outlook*. https://www.imf.org/en/Publications/WEO/weo-database/2020/October. October 2020; and staff calculations.

---

[35] M.A. Kose et al. 2020. Global Waves of Debt: Causes and Consequences. *Finance & Development*. Volume 57. Washington, DC: World Bank.

State aid granted to SOEs due to the pandemic has taken multiple forms including subsidized loans, capital increases, tax and fees deferral, direct grants, and the provision of state guarantees for loans. This support has enabled governments to keep up public services, protect jobs, and supply services and goods after COVID-19 disrupted supply chains. The impact of the debt and fiscal burden will be particularly important for SOEs following COVID-19. Without good design and regulatory oversight, however, emergency support for SOEs can often lead to distortions and weaken transparency and corporate governance. In the medium to long term, contestable markets are necessary to maintain SOE competitiveness, and consumer welfare governments need to be vigilant to avert the risk of crowding out private sector companies, keep inactive SOEs alive, and discourage anticompetitive behavior.

As public resources are scarce, governments need to consider whether support to specific SOEs is an optimal use of limited budgets. Tight fiscal conditions, in conjunction with rising debt in DMCs, makes understanding the issues associated with recording liabilities for infrastructure service provision even more important. Often, SOEs do not adequately monitor and disclose such liabilities. Instead, liabilities may be held off the balance sheet or in off budget funds (such as road funds or other forms of special purpose vehicles), or such liabilities may be based on guarantees. As a result, SOEs wield significant fiscal impacts on the government balance sheet. IMF data, for example, shows that between 1990 and 2014, contingent liabilities of SOEs accounted for 18% of realized liabilities, and fiscal costs from SOE bailouts averaged from 3% to as high as 15% of GDP in the most extreme cases.

The IMF also found that realized liabilities from SOEs were the fourth largest cost related to contingent liabilities after financial systems, legal rulings, and subnational governments. The potential overall fiscal cost of contingent liabilities from all these sources on average was 6% but could reach 40% of GDP for major financial sector bailouts over the study period. Moreover, a contingent liability realization tends to occur during periods of economic growth reversal, putting pressure on budgets already under stress. The study also notes that countries with stronger institutions and fiscal reporting capacity tend to control and manage risks and are less vulnerable to contingent liability crises.[36]

---

36 E. Bolva et al. 2016. *The Impact of Contingent Liability Realizations on Public Finances.* International Monetary Fund. January.

4

QUALITY INFRASTRUCTURE INVESTMENT—KNOWLEDGE PRODUCTS, TOOLS, AND THE INFRASTRUCTURE GOVERNANCE FRAMEWORK

The international development banks and other international bodies have developed infrastructure governance tools, knowledge products, and guidance to help DMCs develop infrastructure that is efficient and sustainable, and to provide access to quality basic services and infrastructure. These tools are helpful but do not replace the effective implementation of a sound governance framework. This involves improving planning capacity to select and design projects that are fiscally sustainable, financed at affordable rates, resilient to corruption, and consistent with government priorities and institutions. Projects that rely on government budgets and debt need to be affordable within the resource constraints of fiscal frameworks. Planning for sustainability means prioritizing multiyear budgets, accounting for all costs over the life of an asset (life-cycle approach) from planning, structuring, and risk allocation to operation and maintenance. An infrastructure governance framework requires coordination across government agencies. The framework should help in identifying, prioritizing, and filtering out the best investments considering the needs and trade-offs associated with a project and with country priorities.

The G20 Hangzhou Summit in September 2016 defined Quality Infrastructure Investment (QII) as investment "which aims to ensure economic efficiency in view of life-cycle cost, safety, resilience against natural hazards, job creation, capacity building, and transfer of expertise and know-how on mutually agreed terms and conditions, while addressing social and environmental impacts and aligning with economic and development strategies."[37]

The G20 leaders affirmed the call for quality infrastructure in endorsing the Principles for QII at the G20 Finance Ministers' and Central Bank Governors' Meeting in Fukuoka, Japan (8–9 June 2019). Their communiqué called for "maximizing the positive impact of infrastructure to achieve sustainable growth and development while preserving the sustainability of public finances, raising economic efficiency in view of life-cycle cost, integrating

---

[37] G20 Leaders Communique. September 2016, Hangzhou.

environmental and social considerations, including women's economic empowerment, building resilience against natural hazards and other risks, and strengthening infrastructure governance."[38]

The Asian Development Fund (ADF) 13th replenishment and the International Development Association (IDA) 19th replenishment view the quantity and the quality of infrastructure investment as important for maximizing the development impact of infrastructure investment.[39]

QII provides a set of general principles but does not give a practical and operational framework useful for DMCs to invest in cost-effective, accessible, and sustainable projects. Improved infrastructure investment management gives considerable benefits throughout a project's life-cycle along with effective coordination between government ministries and national and subnational levels of government. Likewise, the quality of public governance is related to quality of infrastructure and outcomes.[40]

World Bank research found that infrastructure investment costs in lower and middle-income countries vary between 2% and 8% of GDP, subject to the quantity and quality of service plus the spending efficiency realized by investing in and maintaining infrastructure assets. High-quality maintenance can generate significant savings and reduce the life-cycle cost of water, sanitation, and transport infrastructure by more than 50%, demonstrating that upfront investment in infrastructure is not enough; rather, such investments require ongoing maintenance to make infrastructure projects truly sustainable.[41]

ADB, the IMF, the OECD, and the World Bank have produced papers and tools to assess constraints to public infrastructure management and public financial management. Bilateral donors have added to the literature on public investment management (PIM) such as JICA's *Public Investment Management Handbook for Capacity Development* that presents a framework for understanding PIM, analyzing PIM issues and capacity, formulating PIM projects and strategy, and assessing implementation issues.[42] There are diagnostic tools, like PIMA, that can identify gaps in a country's infrastructure governance.

International organizations have developed several assessment tools to improve infrastructure governance like the Tax Administration Assessment and Diagnostic Tool. They have also developed several tools to improve infrastructure governance. The PPP Fiscal Risk Assessment Model produced by the World Bank and IMF is an analytical tool that assesses the risks and fiscal costs of PPP projects.[43] Collectively, these tools help assess and prioritize reforms and increase the overall quality and effectiveness of infrastructure investments. They are used in different jurisdictions but are not widely deployed by countries and differ in their approach. Thus, these tools alone cannot create a coherent framework to guide investments and assess sustainable infrastructure.

SOURCE is a customizable, secure web application for DMC project management, planning, processing, assessment, and overall preparation. Its project management functions include project pipelines, documents, portfolio management, and monitoring dashboards for project preparation, all of which can be tailored to a DMC's regulatory regime and project approval processes. SOURCE project preparation templates provide guidance on

---

38 Available at https://www.mof.go.jp/english/international_policy/convention/g20/annex6_1.pdf. The G20 agreed on six principles:
(i) maximizing the positive impact of infrastructure to achieve sustainable growth and development, (ii) raising economic efficiency in view of life-cycle costs, (iii) integrating environmental considerations in infrastructure investments, (iv) building resilience against natural disasters and other risks, (v) integrating social considerations in infrastructure investment, and(vi) strengthening infrastructure governance.
39 ADB. 2020. *Asia's Journey to Prosperity: Policy, Market, and Technology Over 50 Years.* Chapter 8: Infrastructure Development. Manila.
40 OECD. 2017. *Getting Infrastructure Right: A Framework for Better Governance.* Paris: OECD.
41 S. Hallegatte, J. Rentschler, and J. Rozenberg. 2019. *Lifelines: The Resilient Infrastructure Opportunity.* Washington, DC: World Bank.
42 Japan International Cooperation Agency. 2018. *Public Investment Management Handbook for Capacity Development.*
43 For a list of tools see https://pppknowledgelab.org/tools/ppp-tools-0. Source can be found at https://public.sif-source.org/source/.

managing projects even where the private sector is involved. The SOURCE templates are in accordance with global standards like the IFC performance standards on Environment, Social, and Governance (ESG), the Global Infrastructure Facility (GIF) Project Preparation Readiness Assessment, and the APMG PPP Certification Guide's gateway process. The platform also integrates internationally recognized knowledge products such as the IMF and the World Bank PPP Fiscal Risk Assessment Model that analyzes fiscal risks of infrastructure projects, the GIH PPP risk allocation tool, and the United Nations Environment Programme (UNEP) Principles for Positive Impact Finance.

SOURCE was cited in the G20's InfraTech[44] agenda as a means for countries to enable a systemic transition to the digitalization of infrastructure project preparation and data collection in relation to QII principles. SOURCE helps governments improve investment decisions over a project's life-cycle, enhance value for money, and promote quality infrastructure investments to achieve better economic, social, and environmental outcomes. As a multilateral and online platform, SOURCE holds great potential to digitize and disseminate ADB tools and diagnostic instruments related to infrastructure governance and sustainability, such as the Climate Risk Management Framework, Procurement Risk Assessment, and Value for Money Guidance for Procurement, among others (Table 2). This will enable ADB to expand its knowledge sharing activities and increase DMC access by having tools and best practices available in one place along with knowledge products from other multilaterals.

The key challenge for ADB and other multilateral development banks is how to effectively support the project cycles used by government institutions that plan, allocate resources, and implement public infrastructure investments. This applies to how DMCs carry out project preparation, procurement, environmental and social considerations, and the country policies and regulations that collectively improve the efficiency of traditional public investment and PPPs. ADB can build on this prior body of work and the available assessment by identifying governance constraints to enhance public sector capacity for planning, financing, and delivering quality infrastructure. This requires the bank to build on its existing tools to improve how it supports infrastructure governance in DMCs.

However, even the most carefully structured efforts to address infrastructure governance challenges in DMCs will need political support by committed, reliable, and effective political leaders to ensure implementation. With this support, the bank can build a shared understanding of problems and solutions with DMCs on the quality of infrastructure investment, and more effectively communicate recommendations to key stakeholders. This involves screening projects and identifying which ones are fiscally sustainable and consistent with government priorities. It requires that, within the context of government policies and regulations for public investment, governments improve the institutional capacity for appraising and preparing projects, structuring, and drafting tenders and contracts, procuring, and managing infrastructure assets. In practice, this may require reforming existing government frameworks for project preparation or, in the absence of existing procedures, creating new ones.

When spending more on infrastructure, countries also need to consider how to spend smarter and better to obtain the most value for money. This report points to the relevance of infrastructure governance in improving overall quality and quantity of infrastructure. The key drivers of quality infrastructure are greater sustainability, efficiency, and accessibility. It begins with strengthening institutional capacity to assess fiscal and debt costs; environmental, climate, and disaster risks; and social and economic impacts, and should account for all costs and benefits over the life of an asset (life-cycle costing).

---

44 G20 Infrastructure Working Group. 2020. G20 Riyadh InfraTech Agenda. https://cdn.gihub.org/umbraco/ media/3008/ g20-riyadh-infratech-agenda.pdf.

KEY DRIVERS OF QUALITY INFRASTRUCTURE—EFFICIENCY, ACCESSIBILITY, AND SUSTAINABILITY

Efficiency is the ratio of infrastructure investment capital stock per capita to indicators measuring the quality of and access to infrastructure (footnote 26). DMCs require project selection processes that achieve the greatest social and economic benefits per dollar invested. Efficiency in PPP projects can be measured by the value-for-money (VfM) achieved in a project versus that achieved in a traditional investment. Efficiency focuses on fair and transparent procurement practices that encourage competition to get the best combination of price and value. It requires government capacity to carry out cost–benefit, feasibility, and VfM studies and use these assessments in project evaluation.

Feasibility studies must account for climate and disaster risks, health emergencies, vulnerability to corruption, and uncertainty associated with trends like climate change and hazards. Because pandemics, economic crises, and environmental instability can hit hard and have unpredictable consequences, resilience—the ability to adapt and absorb change and avoid systemic breakdowns—should accompany efficiency and be built into cost–benefit assessments. Governance systems involve multilayered interactions across people, sectors, institutions, and policies; it is therefore important to implement whole-of-government coordination and feedback, including coordination with the private sector and civil society.

Accessibility is based on inclusiveness and responsiveness to increasing inequalities, ensuring infrastructure delivery to the poorest, most remote, and marginalized communities. Project planners need to consult with and consider the needs of affected communities. The design, delivery, and management of infrastructure should consider the needs of all people, especially the most vulnerable like displaced populations, indigenous communities, and individuals with disabilities. For example, authorities should determine how women can best access safe infrastructure, while working toward economic empowerment, including providing equal opportunities for employment created by infrastructure investments. However, one size does not fit all economies when it comes to the design of tariffs.

Depending on project size, private sector development, income levels, and access to finance, traditional PPPs financed by the private sector and supported by user fees may not be practical, particularly in sensitive sectors like water or in low-income communities. While user charges or fees can offset the operational costs of accessible infrastructure, in many cases, governments will still need to budget subsidies for projects to ensure access for the poor. Basic infrastructure from roads to parks represent public goods and are nonexcludable. The use of one individual or group should not limit access for others. Upstream planning and analysis should consider both environmental and social impacts, including access to natural capital by local communities. If not properly anticipated in project design, these social and environmental issues can cause infrastructure-related conflict, often resulting in substantial delays and costs.

Sustainability is based on extending the life of an infrastructure asset; infrastructure projects should build climate and disaster resilience. Many DMC projects are not sufficiently sustainable due to the inherent complexities of infrastructure investment—long time horizons, social impacts, vulnerability to externalities such as climate change, enabling environments, and institutional challenges. Sustainable projects reflect fiscal, economic, environmental, social considerations, climate-resilient design standards, and governance (ESG) aspects. These are part of the 2030 Agenda for Sustainable Development and the Paris Agreement to reduce greenhouse gases and are aligned with national and local development strategies of different countries. A systematic approach requires (i) incorporating environmental sustainability, (ii) capturing and pricing environmental externalities in project appraisal, and (iii) applying safeguards, such as those pertaining to carbon emissions and pollution or energy efficiency.[45]

Governments need to implement sustainable procurement processes that recognize and manage corruption risks and include VfM criteria over project's life. Governments also need to develop more robust planning capacity to select and design projects—both traditional procurement and PPPs—that are fiscally sustainable, financed at affordable rates, resilient to corruption, and consistent with government priorities. Projects that rely on government budgets and debt for infrastructure projects need to be affordable within the resource constraints of fiscal frameworks. Planning for sustainability means prioritizing multiyear budgets, accounting for all costs over the life of an asset (life-cycle approach) from planning, structuring, and risk allocation to operation and maintenance. A sustainable infrastructure program should be whole-of-government, long term, and strategic. This requires coordinating across government agencies and identifying, prioritizing, and filtering out the best investments, considering the needs and trade-offs associated with a project.

---

45 A. Bhattacharya, J. P. Meltzer, Z. Qureshi. 2016. *Delivering on Sustainable Infrastructure for Better Development and Better Climate*. Brookings.

QUALITY INFRASTRUCTURE INVESTMENT— FROM PRINCIPLES TO PRACTICE

PRINCIPLE ONE

Maximizing infrastructure's positive impact to achieve sustainable growth and development. This overarching first principle has elements that apply wholly or in part to other principles. The core message is that a successful infrastructure program should be based on a whole-of-government approach with long-term strategic planning for infrastructure. It should be linked to a transparent and effective public financial management system and to capital budgeting. The performance of the Asia and Pacific region has been mixed, with IMF PIMA scores on overall planning and allocation of resources for infrastructure, on a scale of 1–10, ranging from a low of only 2.7 to a high of 5.6 (footnote 26).

Some countries in Asia and the Pacific, including Cambodia, Fiji, Pakistan, the Philippines, and Thailand, have infrastructure plans that define the infrastructure challenges and opportunities, their government's planned projects, and the priorities for reform and infrastructure investment.[46] However, most do not have whole-of-government planning, and those that do may not consistently implement them. Implementing a sound capital budgeting framework linked to national development needs is essential in ensuring that a country can meet its infrastructure development needs coherently and cost effectively.[47]

---

[46] Global Infrastructure Hub. 2020. InfraCompass.

[47] OECD. 2019. Budgeting and Public Expenditures in OECD Countries. Page 131. The OECD Principles of Budgetary Governance highlight four key elements for infrastructure investment: (i) the grounding of capital investment plans in objective appraisal of economic capacity gaps, infrastructural development needs, and sector/social priorities; (ii) the prudent assessment of costs and benefits of such investments, fiscal affordability and risks, relative priority among various projects, and overall value for money; (iii) the evaluation of investment decisions independently of the specific financing mechanism; and (iv) the development and implementation of a national framework for supporting public investment.

BOX 2	International Monetary Fund on Fiscal Risks and Public–Private Partnerships

Public–private partnerships (PPPs) can create incentives to mobilize private capital and bring in private sector management capacity, but even good PPP projects present some challenges that governments can only mitigate. The recourse to PPP procurement is surrounded by fiscal illusions that prevent careful fiscal risk management and allows for the approval and engagement of too costly or poorly structured projects. There are three main sources of fiscal illusion in PPPs: (i) accounting practices, (ii) asset recognition criteria, and (iii) fiscal risk assessment by public sector contracting agencies.

Accounting practices that allow governments to increase infrastructure without an immediate impact on public sector deficits or debt are a large source of fiscal illusion. Fiscal illusion in PPPs can also arise from failing to recognize PPP assets as public infrastructure. It can also stem from inadequately assessing the fiscal risks in PPP contracts. Weaknesses in infrastructure governance exacerbate fiscal risks. Infrastructure governance comprises the public institutions, processes, and procedures guiding government decisions in planning, allocating funds, and implementing public investment projects, including PPPs. Many fiscal risks in infrastructure originate from weaknesses in the early stages of the project cycle, mainly during strategic planning and project appraisal. By keeping PPPs off-budget, governments can increase long-term commitments in infrastructure without legislative scrutiny or oversight, thereby jeopardizing fiscal sustainability. Inadequate skills and capabilities in public agencies implementing and managing PPPs expose governments to additional risks.

To procure PPPs soundly, governments need to strengthen their infrastructure governance. Further consideration could be given to strengthening the ability of contracting agencies to understand and apply principles associated with Quality Infrastructure Investment, especially given the challenge of assessing risk over a long-term contract. Development agencies need to ensure a more integrated approach to ensure their technical assistance programs work and coordinate with PPP units, finance officials, and infrastructure line ministries that are part of the infrastructure ecosystem.

Source: Manal Fouad et al. 2021. Mastering the Risky Business of Public–Private Partnerships in Infrastructure. *International Monetary Fund Departmental Papers*. No. 2021/010. May.

A recent IMF reference note (Box 2) highlights the importance of fiscal costs and risks associated with PPPs. The reference note defines the "fiscal illusion" of PPPs, sources of fiscal risks, and the role of infrastructure governance in managing fiscal risk. Critical governance elements include

(i) a gateway process governing the preparation and procurement of PPP projects with a strong role of the ministry of finance;

(ii) a proactive fiscal risk management function for PPPs in the ministry of finance;

(iii) budgeting, accounting, and reporting standards and practices that ensure fiscal transparency regarding PPPs; and

(iv) an enabling legal framework that is clear and consistent.

The inability of many governments to identify, price, and manage PPP risks hinders effective implementation of this gateway process and the ability to address this fiscal illusion squarely. From a broader economic and fiscal management perspective, this constrains a government's ability to determine the optimal level of guarantees and other forms of contingent liabilities in PPP contracts. This is a fundamental challenge in addressing the value for money proposition and the foundations of PPP contracting.

PRINCIPLE TWO

Raising economic efficiency in view of life-cycle cost. Raising the economic efficiency of infrastructure requires that project appraisals include VfM, life-cycle costs, fiscal sustainability, affordability, risk assessment, allocation, and mitigation, as well as innovative technology with the potential to be more cost-effective and resilient. Efficiency refers to the allocation of resources to select projects that generate optimum social and economic returns to society. In line with the life-cycle approach, rehabilitation/renewal also serves as a critical component when considering the economic efficiency of infrastructure assets.

VfM as part of procurement strategy increases efficiency by considering quantitative life-cycle costs and the qualitative economic costs and benefits to society. ADB issued guidance notes to address these separately. The *Guidance Note on Strategic Procurement Planning* assists DMCs in developing procurement strategies and procurement plans for loan and grant projects financed by ADB.[48] The *Guidance Note on Value for Money* defines VfM as the effective, efficient, and economic use of resources. This ADB definition is broadly similar, conceptually, to how VfM for PPPs is understood, applied, and measured. Both the ADB guidance note on VfM and VfM as applied to PPPs require an evaluation of costs and benefits along with all relevant risks, non-price attributes, and the total cost of ownership of an asset.

Effectively applying the VfM principle may reduce risk and improve quality when authorities identify and manage risks and apply life-cycle costing and sound evaluation criteria. VfM also improves performance by encouraging more cost-effective and innovative solutions to meet identified needs and contributes to a better balance of costs and benefits throughout project delivery.

ADB's *Guidelines for Economic Analysis of Projects* underpins value for money analyses. Key principles of economic analysis are related to life-cycle costing and VfM analyses in assessing infrastructure efficiency as part of ADB's due diligence requirements for project preparation. According to these guidelines, first, an economically viable project should embody the most efficient and least cost option to achieve the intended project outcomes; second, the economic surplus should be above project opportunity cost; and third, O&M should have sufficient funding to ensure fiscal, socioeconomic, and environmental sustainability in line with the project's objectives.

Best global practices typically subject potential capital investments to rigorous economic analysis, with decision makers prioritizing and funding what is economically viable within a country's medium-term budget framework. Economically viable projects should be considered in a country's infrastructure financing plan and subsequent procurement decisions should come after assessing which delivery method—PPP or a traditional public option—will more likely achieve project objectives for quality infrastructure.

Among the key factors leading to inadequate water and sanitation systems, unreliable electricity grids, and overstrained transport networks are lack of funding and poor infrastructure maintenance. A World Bank analysis of OECD countries shows that each additional $1 spent on road maintenance saves $1.50 in new investments, demonstrating that maintenance is cost-effective.[49] According to ADB, poor roads can raise annual vehicle operating costs by around $2–$3 per vehicle-kilometer.[50] A life-cycle approach covers the lifespan of a project, including capital investment for construction, O&M, and renewal of investments over time. An example of incorporating life-cycle costs is the Philippines' Clark International Airport PPP. This innovative, hybrid PPP

---

48   ADB. 2018. *Value for Money: Guidance Note on Procurement*. June. Manila.
49   S. Hallegatte, J. Rentschler, and J. Rozenberg. 2019. *Lifelines: The Resilient Infrastructure Opportunity*. World Bank.
50   ADB. 2003. *Road Funds and Road Maintenance: An Asian Perspective*. Manila.

signed in 2019 is a 25-year concession—the first airport project in the Philippines to be tendered under the Philippine government's hybrid PPP policy.[51] The concession involves equipping, managing, and maintaining the entire Clark Airport facility constructed under an EPC contract that concluded in 2017.

E-procurement can streamline procurement decision-making and make it less prone to corruption with the primary benefit being transparency in the infrastructure space. It increases efficiency by integrating the procurement process with other government accountability and budget systems, like the asset register, general ledger, budget, and accounts payable. It can increase the functionality of these systems while increasing the transparency and accountability of the procurement process through online publication and disclosure of critical documents such as procurement opportunities and plans. A cross-government e-procurement system can deliver greater VfM by minimizing process duplication among different agencies. It can provide supplier efficiencies and leverage government buying power through framework agreements.[52] However, the greatest transactional benefits of such systems are the consolidation of low-value repeatable transactions rather than infrastructure procurement.

Innovative technologies like drones, sensors, and the Internet of Things can raise economic efficiency and increase VfM. While infrastructure plays a transformative role across industries, the infrastructure sector has yet to fully exploit the potential of these technologies to reduce costs and improve quality. The adoption of innovative technology could close the financing gap and promote sustainable and inclusive growth. Examples include sensors in transportation projects to monitor traffic flow and patterns thereby helping to reduce time and traffic congestion. In the water sector, utilities can identify potential lost revenue due to water leakage using sensors. These may incur increased expenditure during installation and adaptation but can eventually save money and improve efficiency.

Making decision-makers aware in real-time of the need for repair and replacement can increase overall resiliency. In the energy sector, technology can overcome constraints to improve grid infrastructure, making it stronger, more resilient, and smarter. Artificial Intelligence (AI) can help create smart cities and make transport systems and buildings more "intelligent" by reducing energy consumption for the same level of services, comfort, and mobility. For example, at a time when project supervisors cannot get to the field due to COVID-19 risks, drones help reduce personal safety risks by facilitating remotely performed inspections. Big data can also play a role in tracking the pandemic's impact on traffic patterns (Box 3). Even after the pandemic and social distancing ends, remote inspections should continue to benefit transit agencies and the traveling public. Moreover, the cost of drone inspection has already decreased by almost 40%.[53] Though new technologies carry new risks such as procurement regulations that may limit their adoption, COVID-19 could encourage their adoption and accelerate production automation.

---

[51] IFC. 2019. Contracts Signed for Clark International Airport Expansion and Modernization, Pioneering Hybrid PPP. Press Release. 6 February.

[52] ADB. 2018. *E-Procurement – Guidance Note on Procurement*. Manila. This guidance note explains how ADB encourages the use of electronic procurement (e-procurement) in different stages of the procurement process. It describes the benefits of e-procurement and the tools ADB uses in assessing systems, suggesting possible approaches to its implementation.

[53] A. Falk et al. 2020. *Transportation Infrastructure and COVID-19 A Moment that Matters*. 22 May. New York: Deloitte.

BOX 3	Using Big Data to Track the Pandemic

ADB analyzed transport data showing the relationship between urban mobility and coronavirus disease (COVID-19). Transportation patterns are changing as countries emerge from COVID-19.

Using data from popular GPS mobility apps, the study revealed a decrease in ridership of almost 90% in Southeast Asia in comparison with pre-pandemic patterns in January 2020. This was mainly due to lockdowns and social distancing measures governments imposed. The biggest transport reduction was in Kuala Lumpur registering a decline of 94.2%. The Philippines saw a drop in the flow of traffic of around 94% in Metro Manila, Cebu City, and Davao City. Overall mobility and the use of public transport gradually returned to normal as cities returned to normal.

More study is required to understand the impact on modes of travel, origins and destinations, and human contacts. This study however shows the importance of open data to help cities plan and implement resilient mobility solutions. It is also important to safeguard ethical sharing of mobility information between the public and the private sector.

Source: ADB and Thinking Machines. Bruno Carrasco et al.. 2021. Mapping Digital Poverty in the Philippines using AI, Big Data and Machine Learning. 1 Feb. https://stories.thinkingmachin.es/mapping-digital-poverty-in-the-philippines/.

PRINCIPLE THREE

Integrating environmental considerations in infrastructure investments. This principle highlights the importance of incorporating social and environmental mitigation measures and innovative green finance to ensure projects are environmentally sound. Project stakeholders (i.e., government agencies, investors, and EPC contractors) should note economic developments, demographic shifts, climate change impacts (including the risk of stranded assets if larger climate risks and commitments are not accommodated), relationships with local communities, and the policy and legislative framework at the earliest stages of infrastructure development. Likewise, major ESG issues that can impact commercial viability, the approval of licenses, and necessary timelines must also be addressed at this stage. Infrastructure planners should consider the impact of negative externalities like health and safety incidents and environmental damages indirectly related to a project that may negatively impact an investment. Environmental safeguards emphasize minimizing and/or managing the impacts of a project on the environment (an externality). This is distinct from climate resilience, which focuses on minimizing and/or managing climate impact on projects and the services they deliver.

All major multilateral development banks recognize the importance of policies governing the environmental and social impacts of projects. The safeguard process should be as efficient as possible to reduce time and costs. Although it is hard to pin down the value of safeguards, the benefits outweigh the costs in the long run.[54] An evaluation of ADB safeguard policies found them satisfactory in helping avoid, minimize, and mitigate adverse project impacts related to the environment and involuntary resettlement, and identified areas for improvement. The evaluation found limited policy customization for private sector operations, especially for small island developing economies and fragile and conflict-affected economies; limited guidance for different lending modalities (such as financial intermediation and general corporate finance); weak integration between environmental and social safeguards; insufficient focus on risk management for vulnerable groups and indigenous peoples; limited functionality of project-level grievance redress mechanisms; and insufficient use of technologies and innovation for assessment, monitoring, consultation, and disclosure.[55]

Principle three supports the integration of environmental considerations into innovative green finance instruments that can help expand government funds for financing green infrastructure (i.e., environmentally benign or beneficial infrastructure). These include, for example, pay-for-success financing models (payment based on results), land value capture (recover and reinvest increases in land value resulting from public investment) enabling governments to finance infrastructure investment, or recycling capital (selling or leasing brownfield assets and concessions and using the revenue earned to finance greenfield infrastructure).

The Washington, DC Water and Sewer Authority (DC Water) is an example of how a well-designed disaster risk finance scheme can provide incentives for green infrastructure by financing preventive measures, as its Environmental Impact Bond (EIB) financed the construction of a nature-based storm water facility. This pay-for-success bond provided investment capital payable based on achievement by the private provider of agreed upon results. The pay-for-success model allowed the EIB to raise capital for the environmental program, with payments to the private provider based on the achievement of measured outcomes. Investors receive a premium on the interest rate if the project exceeds targets and a reduction in payment if the project underperforms against the agreed upon targets.[56]

Private investors, including institutional investors representing an enormous reservoir of potential investments, are increasingly valuing ESG in investment decisions. Moody's, Standard & Poor's, and Fitch rating agencies have been providing ESG scores since 2019 for private investors to easily identify risk-adjusted investment opportunities (see Box 4).[57] The European Parliament and European Union member states have agreed to a new sustainability disclosure requirement to encourage more private investors to consider ESG criteria when they assess companies.

Another framework is the Principles for Responsible Investment, signed on to by a UN-supported network of investment managers and asset owners, representing $70 trillion in assets, committing to apply ESG principles in their businesses and investments. This requires signatories to report on their responsible investment activities. FAST-Infra (conceived by the Climate Policy Initiative, HSBC, the International Finance Corporation, OECD, and the Global Infrastructure Facility) is a platform with 100 participating institutions developing a sustainable

54 P. Landragan. 2018. The Health and Economic Benefits of Climate Mitigation and Pollution Control. *The Lancet: Planetary Health*. Volume 2, Issue 3. E107–E108. 1 Mar. The main finding is ..." the health and economic co-benefits achieved through reductions in levels of air pollution and pollution-related disease significantly outweigh the costs of mitigation. These benefits remained evident in sensitivity analyses. The most favorable cost–benefit ratios were in India and the PRC, but benefits outweigh costs in all geographic regions. Another important finding was that the additional expense required to achieve a 1.5°C climate mitigation target will generate a net benefit substantially greater than that associated with the achievement of a 2.0°C target, especially in the PRC and India."
55 ADB. 2020. *Corporate Evaluation: Effectiveness of the 2009 Safeguard Policy Statement*. Manila.
56 OECD. 2018. Climate Resilient Infrastructure: Policy Perspectives, *OECD Environment Policy Paper*. No.14. Paris.
57 Moody's Investor Service. 2017. Moody's Approach to Assessing ESG in Credit Analysis.

BOX 4	**Moody's Methodology for Assessing Environmental, Social, and Governance in Credit Analysis**

Environmental, social, and governance (ESG) analysis has been increasingly mainstreamed by the investment community in the past decade. ESG analysis helps investors minimize risks and protect investment portfolios. Moody's defined ESG as "qualitative and quantitative performance indicators that assess the sustainability and ethical impact of an organization's businesses or investments, such as managing a company's carbon footprint, or ensuring management accountability."

Credit analysis for corporations evaluates ESG impacts on financial strength, reputation, demand for products and services, and production costs. It also considers other long-term impacts that may not currently affect business financials and stability but can in the future. Long-term impacts that are not measurable are included as qualitative considerations. In the ESG ratings of sovereigns, credit analysis assesses potential impacts on government effectiveness, rule of law, competitiveness, political risk, and corruption. The methodology scorecard assesses material impacts on economic and institutional strength, fiscal sustainability, and resiliency.

Some emerging sovereign markets have potential exposure to climate and natural hazards. Moody's has also developed an assessment framework evaluating the potential impact of climate change on sovereign credit ratings for countries most vulnerable to such risks. It measures the physical effects of climate change on an economy by the degree of susceptibility to climate change risk. This looks at exposure based on economic diversification and geographic resiliency considering a country's development level, fiscal flexibility, and government policies.

Source: Moody's Investor Service, 2017 Environmental, Social and Governance (ESG) – Global: Moody's Approach to Assessing ESG in Credit Analysis.

infrastructure label, as well as platforms for targeted financial interventions.[58] While there are many companies doing ratings, such frameworks are nascent and without standardization, and need to be continuously monitored so that ESG considerations are entrenched throughout the entire life-cycle of infrastructure projects along with environmental regulations to encourage green investment in the private and public sectors.

ADB published a technical note to support a "build back better" approach to restore green economic growth, build resilience, and improve long-term quality of life. The note highlights how specific recovery interventions in the context of COVID-19 can support low-carbon development that improves resiliency to climate change and disasters. It gives decision makers a set of policy interventions maximizing climate resiliency and sustainable economic growth (Box 5).

---

[58] B. Buchner et al. 2021. FAST-Infra. Climate Poligy Initiative. Blog. 1 March. See https://www.climatepolicyinitiative.org/fast-infra/.

BOX 5	ADB: Promoting Climate and Disaster Resilience and Low-Carbon Development in COVID-19 Recovery

Adopting a low-carbon and resilient recovery program can be cost effective and accomplished within existing investments. Past crises reveal several characteristics that will support "good" economic recovery from coronavirus disease (COVID-19), usually focusing on job creation and economic stimulation. They have a short implementation timeline, are labor intensive, promote skills development like re-skilling those from sectors heavily impacted by COVID-19 and preparing them for a low-carbon future, have a strong local and diversified supply chain, and have high economic multipliers.

The scale of COVID-19 and the accompanying response means decisions made today will affect and define development directions. ADB developing member countries (DMCs) should consider recovery as an opportunity to reorient their economies towards a low carbon future. Simultaneously, they should address climate and disaster resilience and underlying vulnerabilities across sectors and local communities. An ADB technical note shows a range of interventions that can achieve recovery goals by investing in green projects resulting in positive economic and social benefits while contributing to climate mitigation and resiliency. For example, building insulation retrofits or clean energy infrastructure delivers high economic multipliers, is labor intensive, and can have high returns over the long term by reducing the cost of clean energy. The note cites evidence-based economic data showing that spending $1 million produces 7.49 full-time jobs in renewables infrastructure, and 7.72 full-time jobs in energy efficiency, but only 2.65 full-time jobs for fossil fuels. Recent estimates show that the net benefit of resilient infrastructure investment in low- and middle-income countries leads to $4 in benefits for each $1 invested.

A key feature of the technical note is a proposed assessment framework to prioritize and select investment packages that maximize economic growth while promoting a climate-resilient recovery. The framework identifies specific recovery measures, potential climate and resiliency benefits, and their relation to COVID-19 recovery. It shows whether an activity has a short implementation timeframe while showing its impact on employment, skill development, and the supply chain; its economic multiplier; the associated increase in productive assets; its transformational impacts; and the positive social and environmental outcomes.

The assessment framework can assist DMCs to evaluate investments in low-carbon and disaster-resilient investments needed to restore economic growth. For example, a carbon tax would have a long-term transformational impact on energy, a high economic multiplier, and positive environmental and social outcomes, but would limit short-term employment in the affected sector. Workers may need to be re-skilled so they can be employed in sectors experiencing increased demand over the medium term. The framework can enable a rapid assessment or serve as the basis for a more in-depth analysis for each phase of recovery. The framework is an input into decision-making for investment planning and should meet the specific circumstances of each DMC's economic recovery plan. ADB can play an essential role in assisting DMCs to plan and implement their recovery, plan their institutional and policy reforms, and integrate these into country partnership strategies.

Source: ADB. 2020. *Promoting Climate and Disaster Resilience and Low Carbon Development in the COVID-19 Recovery*. Manila.

ADB's Green Bond program supports innovative green finance in five priority areas: clean energy, sustainable transport, forestry and land-use management for carbon sequestration, climate resiliency, and support for institutional and governance capacities.[59] The program has raised over $5 billion in financing to support ADB projects.

---

[59] ADB. 2019. *Green Bond Newsletter and Impact Report*. Manila.

Building resilience against natural disasters and other risks. The concept of building resilience goes beyond ESG analysis. Planners should assess climate and disaster risks, including geophysical risks like earthquakes, as part of the selection and appraisal of projects. They should identify solutions that enhance the resilience of infrastructure systems and align these with low-carbon objectives. An analysis of the risk of disasters triggered by natural hazards needs to be included in the design of infrastructure and in the preparation of a disaster risk management plan. ADB estimates that the cost of climate change to Southeast Asia could be as much as 11% of GDP by 2100 due to impacts on agriculture, tourism, health, ecosystems, and labor productivity, and because of catastrophic risks.[60] The average net benefit of investing in more resilient infrastructure in DMCs is $4.2 trillion globally, with $4 in benefit for each $1 invested, according to the World Bank report, *Lifelines: The Resilient Infrastructure Opportunity*.

In some cases, there are institutional or policy barriers to incorporating climate and disaster resilience in infrastructure projects.[61] Many countries have national design standards based on historic weather extremes that do not take the changing climate into account. During the preparation of its Northeastern Provinces Sector Project in Viet Nam, ADB adjusted the existing road design parameters to account for expected changes in future extreme rainfall events based on changing climate patterns. The bank worked with the government to update and adjust the national design standards for a changing climate. The analyses translated projections into climate "safety margins" for standard variables such as heavy precipitation, sea-level rise, and river flow.[62]

Since 2014, ADB has put in place a climate risk management framework to provide the basis for systematically screening all ADB investments for climate risk, and for projects with medium and high screening results to undertake climate risk and adaptation assessment as part of project preparation. The bank produced a working paper on climate risk management for climate proofing projects, underscoring the importance of integrating climate considerations into projects from conception to implementation and setting out guiding principles for climate risk management at every stage (Box 6). Such principles become equally critical as ADB aims to align its operation with the goals of the Paris Agreement.

---

[60] ADB. 2016. *Southeast Asia and the Economics of Global Climate Stabilization.* Manila. https://www.adb.org/publications/southeast-asia-economics-global-climate-stabilization.

[61] ADB. 2017. *Disaster Risk Assessment for Project Preparation: A Practical Guide.* This document provides guidance to facilitate the consideration of disaster risks in the design of development projects.

[62] P. Watkiss, R. Wilby, and C.A. Rogers. 2020. Principles of Climate Risk Management for Climate Proofing Projects. *ADB Sustainable Development Working Paper Series.* No. 69. Manila.

BOX 6	Principles of Climate Risk Management for Climate Proofing Projects

Principle 1: Identify climate change risks for regions, sectors, and communities in the country partnership strategy to inform and support the development of a pipeline of adaptation projects and climate proofing activities.

Principle 2: Identify the types of climate proofing projects and their suitability for light-touch assessment considering the project lifetime, degree of lock-in, level of precaution needed, and project size at the concept stage. Type 1 projects focus on climate proofing of proposed investments suitable for light-touch climate assessment or a more in-depth assessment where climate risks are highly material. Type 2 projects focus on climate adaptation where addressing climate risks is the primary objective (e.g., coastal protection to manage rising sea levels).

Principle 3: Identify what matters, understanding key climate risks that can affect the project objectives and outcomes in the preparation phase.

Principle 4: Source targeted climate information, focusing on key risk metrics using light-touch assessment and sensitivity testing to determine the selection and use of climate information during the preparation stage.

Principle 5: Identify adaptation options, given the timing and the degree of uncertainty.

Principle 6: Include activities that enable more flexible and iterative adaptation and enhance mechanisms for monitoring, evaluation, and learning during implementation.

Source: P. Watkiss, R. Wilby, and C.A. Rogers. 2020. Principles of Climate Risk Management for Climate Proofing Projects. *ADB Sustainable Development Working Paper Series.* No. 69. Manila.

With COVID-19 and the state of the climate crisis, the OECD and the G20, among others, have underscored the idea of "building back better" as part of green stimulus packages for countries coming out of economic recession after the pandemic. The OECD policy brief *Building Back Better: A Sustainable, Resilient Recovery after COVID-19* argues that sound policies and investments in climate-resilient and low-carbon infrastructure can reduce the economic severity of future disasters and increase resilience to respond to shocks that do happen.[63] A World Bank study showed that infrastructure investment based on full decarbonization does not necessarily cost more than polluting alternatives, depending on the level of efficiency, policy choices, and technology.[64]

However, the financing scenario is different due to COVID-19; estimates of spending on green development projects as a percentage of GDP have sharply declined and risk perception has increased as governments reallocate budgets to large emergency relief programs. Nevertheless, an Oxford Smith School of Enterprise and the Environment study shows evidence of high economic multipliers for green investments. As noted in Box 5, an investment of $1 million creates 7.49 full-time jobs in renewable energy infrastructure, and 7.72 full-time

---

[63] OECD. 2020. *Building Back Better: A Sustainable, Resilient Recovery after COVID-19.* Paris.
[64] Presentation by Vivian Foster. 2019. Third Roundtable on Infrastructure Governance Republic of Korea, May.

jobs in energy efficiency, but only 2.65 full-time jobs in fossil fuels.[65] These public investments offer high returns and promote green innovation in the infrastructure sector with spillover to the wider economy though they may be challenging to implement, especially when governments face large debts and reduced revenues due to COVID-19.

Governments need private and public investment for green infrastructure projects, especially for poorer countries or small island economies facing higher risk perceptions. An example is the Enhancing Safety, Security, and Sustainability of Apia Port Project in Samoa, financed by a $62 million ADB grant. This project will improve the efficiency, safety, and environmental sustainability of Samoa's primary port, while including a TA component to develop insurance options to protect against climate events (Box 7).

ADB increased climate financing considerably from 2011 to 2019 (Figure 14), committing to integrating climate change mitigation and adaptation in 75% of its sovereign and nonsovereign operations, based on a 3-year rolling average, by 2030.[66]

BOX 7	Samoa's Apia Port: Climate Resilience and Adaptation

ADB provided a grant for the Apia Port in Samoa to develop insurance options that respond to climate and disaster risks. Risks associated with natural hazards, climate change, and other shocks (such as pandemics, terrorism, or shipping accidents) will be evaluated.

Modeling this risk will quantify the socioeconomic implications caused by physical damages and operational interruptions and analyze the cost–benefit of risk reduction measures. It will also identify investments to enhance resilience and climate adaption and options for transferring remaining residual risks to private insurers. Integrating risk transfer options as part of comprehensive risk management will make adaptation investments more sustainable and further reduce the volatility of the government budget against unexpected disaster events.

The grant will also leverage the value proposition of insurance for other state-owned enterprises in Samoa, which may lead to risk pooling solutions across various state-owned enterprise assets. This model has applicability for other Pacific island countries to pool risks at a regional level, backed by international reinsurance structures. This can enhance the region's overall resilience to disaster events and promote regional integration.

Source: ADB. 2019. ADB, Samoa Partner to Enhance Safety, Security of Apia Port. News release. 10 September. https://www.adb.org/news/adb-samoa-partner-enhance-safety-security-apia-port.

---

[65] ADB. 2020. *Green Finance Strategies for Post-COVID-19 Economic Recovery in Southeast Asia.* Manila.
[66] ADB. 2018. *Strategy 2030: Achieving a Prosperous, Inclusive, Resilient and Sustainable Asia and the Pacific.* Manila.

Figure 14: Growth of ADB Climate Financing 2011–2019
(including external cofinancing, $ million)

Year	Mitigation	Adaptation
2011	2,420	757
2012	2,388	896
2013	2,280	988
2014	2,137	719
2015	2,561	356
2016	3,250	1,187
2017	4,236	998
2018	2,725	1,286
2019	5,537	1,536

Legend: Mitigation; Adaptation; Target financing by 2020

Source: Asian Development Bank (2020).

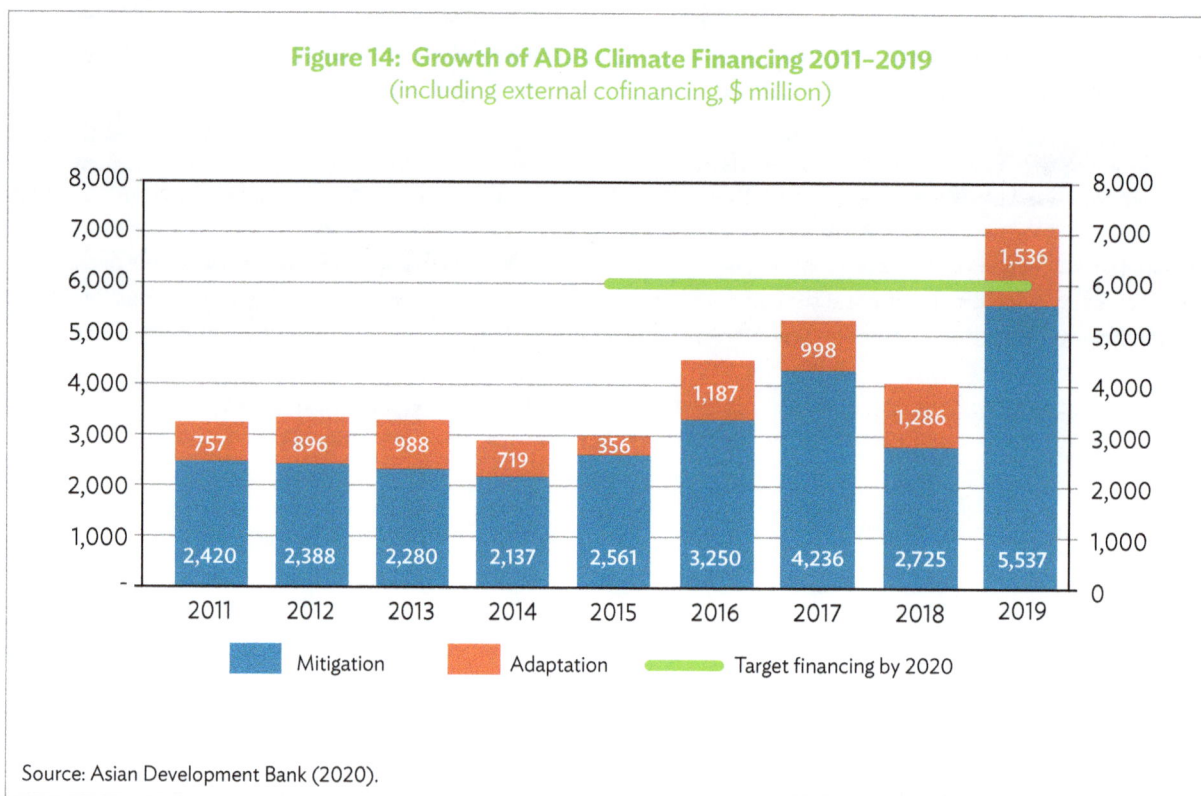

ADB's draft discussion paper on *Green Finance Strategies for Post-COVID-19 Economic Recovery in Southeast Asia* presents finance mechanisms and concepts for green recovery plans of DMCs. The paper highlights how governments can use and de-risk investment while accelerating the development of capital markets for green infrastructure (Box 8).[67] Restoring damaged ecosystems and protecting natural areas can also have positive economic impacts. For example, protecting 30% of forests and mangroves globally would have avoided losses valued between $170 billion and $534 billion annually by 2050. Economic benefits stem from avoiding damage caused by soil loss, coastal storm damage, and flooding.[68]

A hospital to be constructed in Xiangtan, Hunan Province, People's Republic of China, is in a critical flood-prone zone. ADB supported the analysis of urban hazards and challenges, urban climate resilience, adaptation planning, and nature-based solutions, including ecosystem-based adaptation measures to ensure resilient construction. Initiatives that resulted from this analysis included converting trees to tree pits, rain gardens for stormwater runoff as well as modifying porous pavement for cycle lanes and pedestrian walkway using subsurface infiltration for water storage below the pedestrian walkways and bicycle paths. These measures reduce runoff pollution, and decrease peak volume stormwater for flood protection and resistance to droughts, and improve overall urban aesthetics.[69]

---

[67] ADB. 2020. *Green Finance Strategies for Post-COVID-19 Economic Recovery in Southeast Asia.* Manila.
[68] *Development Asia.* 2020. Letting Nature Regrow is the World Banes Hope for a Healthy Future. 17 December. https://development.asia/insight/letting-nature-regrow-worlds-best-hope-healthy-future.
[69] F. van de Ven, R. Brolsma, and Na Won Kim. 2020. *How Ecosystem-Based Solutions Can Develop Climate-Resilient Cities. Development Asia.* Manila: Asian Development Bank.

BOX 8	Green Finance Strategies for Post COVID-19 Economic Recovery in Southeast Asia: Draft for Discussion

Green finance combines leveraged finance mechanisms and public sector funds to attract private capital for every dollar of public sector funding spent, with green indicators and targets for supported projects. Putting green infrastructure development at the core of a country's economic recovery strategy is critical to achieving equitable and sustainable development. Infrastructure development creates jobs and economic growth for the long term.

The greatest challenge to green infrastructure development across Southeast Asia is the lack of adequate funds flowing into the sector. Southeast Asia will need around $3.1 trillion for climate resilient infrastructure but has an estimated financing gap of $210 billion annually. Private sector financing to fill the infrastructure gap—often ranging from 50% to 90%—is needed. The coronavirus (COVID-19) pandemic has altered the availability of public finance as governments divert budgetary resources to large emergency relief programs. The risk profile of green infrastructure is perceived to be high risk due to new technology, higher capital costs and operating expenses, and commercial banks that are not familiar with these types of investments. The Asian Development Bank (ADB) supports developing member countries to create financing opportunities through its expertise in financial structuring and by offering concessional funds that can de-risk projects and encourage private investment.

Examples include the Shandong Green Development Fund financing mechanism of $1.5 billion created with ADB support in the Shandong Province of the People's Republic of China. The fund blends finance from commercial and institutional sources for green investments while other potential financial options include green bonds supported by risk assurances provided by governments and multilateral development banks. In addition to traditional green bonds, there is a potential to structure specific COVID-19 green bonds for sovereigns, state-owned enterprises, and local governments that support investment projects with positive climate impacts especially for sectors impacted by COVID-19.

Source: ADB. 2020. Green Finance Strategies for Post-COVID-19 Economic Recovery in Southeast Asia. Draft for Internal Discussion Only, Asian Green Finance Catalytic Facility. June.

Asia is the most populated region of the world with growing demand for natural resources and energy. The region is also the biggest emitter of greenhouse gases, and the region's ability to respond to this challenge will have a global impact. The energy sector's development will have significant implications on climate and long-lasting impact on regional economic development. In the context of ADB's Strategy 2030, ADB's Independent Evaluation Department analyzed the Energy Policy from 2009 to 2019 to contribute to a new energy policy and steer future operations prioritizing climate change mitigation and adaptation (Box 9).

The World Bank in 2017 issued the first specialized bonds providing financing for the Pandemic Emergency Financing Facility. The purpose was to channel rapid funding to developing countries confronted by a pandemic. The bonds were issued after the 2013–2016 Ebola outbreak in Liberia, Sierra Leone, and Guinea. However, the complex design of the bonds caused a prolonged delay in meeting the criteria for a payout after the outbreak of COVID-19.

BOX 9	Sector-Wide Evaluation: ADB Energy Policy and Program, 2009–2019

This evaluation aims to develop lessons learned and make recommendations to the Asian Development Bank's (ADB's) Management and Board to inform a revision of the Energy Policy in line with Strategy 2030. From 2009 to 2019, the energy sector accounted for $42.5 billion in approvals, the second largest sector of ADB approvals.

The transmission and distribution subsector, and conventional and renewable generation, supported developing member countries (DMCs) to decrease or eliminate power shortages and improve affordability and reliability. On the other hand, the program was not as effective in meeting other needs like demand-side efficiency, capacity-building and governance, reforms in the energy sector, promoting regional cooperation and investments in resilience, and climate proofing of energy infrastructure. Although renewable energy investments were relatively modest, these were often first-time projects with demonstrable impacts facilitating a reduction in risk perception and attracting private investors into the sector. The evaluation identified the need to improve project quality: only 21% of the 66 approved sovereign loans had on-time performance, and 42% experienced delays of 2 or more years. During project preparation, the focus was on Board approval, but when it came to project supervision, more attention was focused on outputs and disbursements than on outcome indicators, project results, and impacts. More work will be needed to foster internal collaboration and the "One ADB" approach, and the transition to a "knowledge bank" will need to continue. The evaluation indicates an excessive focus on project approvals over quality.

The evaluation recommended an update to the Energy Policy with greater focus on climate mitigation and adaptation, suggesting also a withdrawal from financing greenfield and major rehabilitations of coal-fired power and heat generation projects, in line with ADB's practice since 2013. The evaluation suggested high-level engagement in support of DMC's long-term sector plans for integrated energy planning, taking into consideration economic development, environmental sustainability, and energy security to maximize regional resources while addressing climate change, increasing knowledge creation and dissemination, strengthening collaboration with the Asian Development Bank Institute and outside knowledge partners, and promoting innovation.

Source: ADB. 2020. *Sector-wide Evaluation: ADB Energy Policy and Program, 2009–2019*. Evaluation Document. 20 August.

PRINCIPLE FIVE

Integrating social considerations in infrastructure investment. This principle refers to consultation with affected communities and stakeholders and inclusive decision-making from planning to implementation. This is key to securing equitable access for users of infrastructure, especially for vulnerable populations like women and children, persons with disabilities, indigenous communities, and impoverished and marginalized populations. Digital access and connectivity by poor communities is even more important as populations now deal with social distancing and lockdowns. ADB and the technology firm, Thinking Machines, used machine learning technology to digitally map spatial patterns of inequality overlaid with internet download speeds at the city level (Figure 15). The map legend colors from left to right show decreasing wealth and increasing poverty levels; the colors from the bottom up show faster download speeds. The more affluent areas of Metro Manila, Central Luzon, and Cebu in the Philippines represent faster speeds in pink. The dark colors in the upper right hand of the legend represent low wealth and slower download speeds.

Figure 15: Internet Speeds and Wealth Index for Philippine Cities and Municipalities

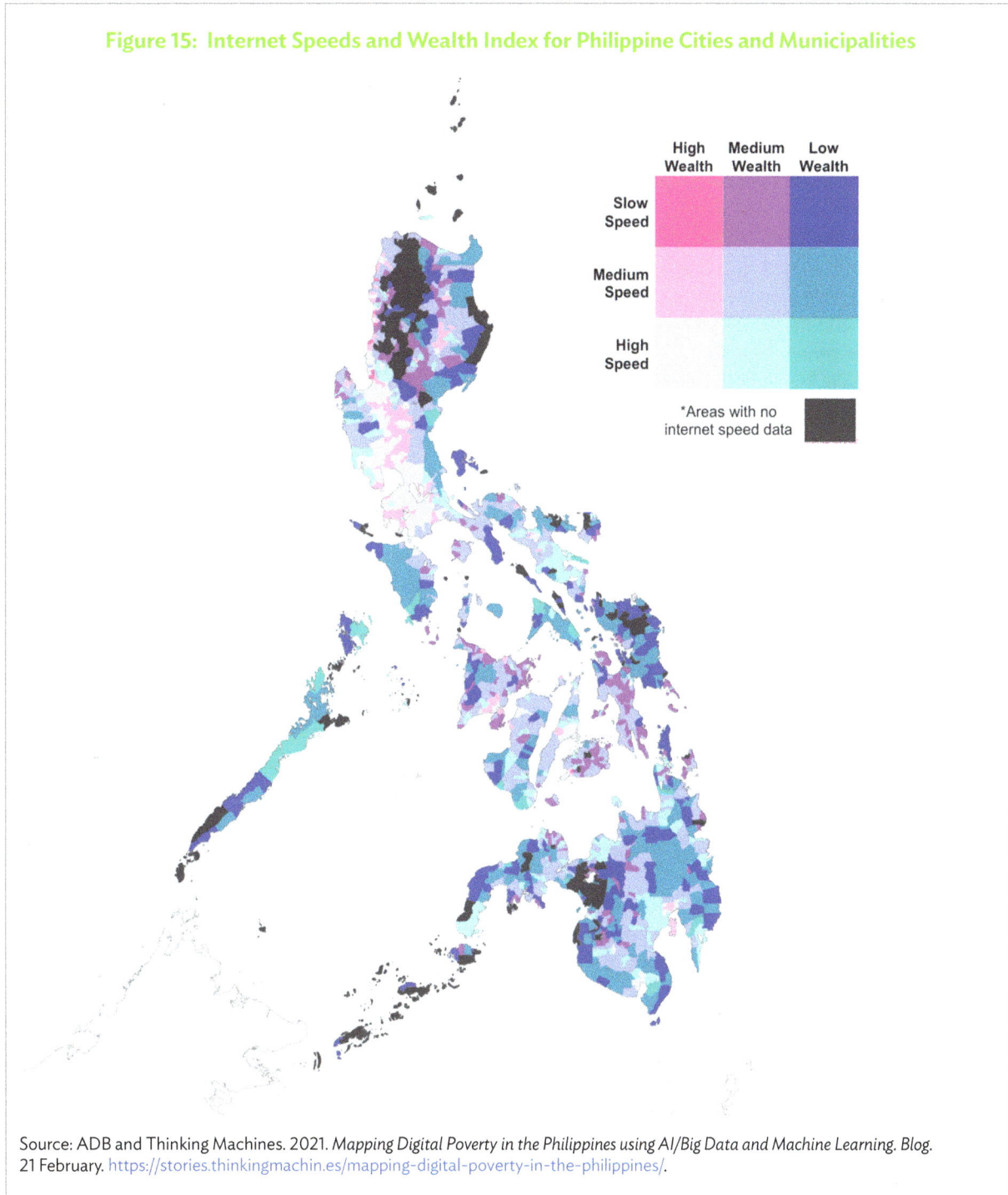

Source: ADB and Thinking Machines. 2021. *Mapping Digital Poverty in the Philippines using AI/Big Data and Machine Learning. Blog.*
21 February. https://stories.thinkingmachin.es/mapping-digital-poverty-in-the-philippines/.

It is also necessary to ensure safe and healthy occupational conditions at the infrastructure site and surrounding communities. An ADB paper proposed a framework for effective multistakeholder engagement that institutions can apply to develop infrastructure projects. The framework defines effective stakeholder engagement along a number of dimensions including listening to dissenting voices, transparency in designing and implementing change interventions, and supporting institutional mechanisms that promote transparency and disclose and disseminate project information.[70] From an operational perspective, this means building a consultation process into the project cycle, from initial project screening and identification to project implementation, and holding relevant government officials accountable for integrating this feedback into decision-making.

PRINCIPLE SIX

Strengthening infrastructure governance. This principle broadly covers project cycle governance, from procurement to operations and asset management. It seeks to ensure that the procurement framework and decision-making processes from launching a bid to evaluating, awarding, and managing projects are well defined, fair, transparent, and competitive. This framework should consider the impact of contingent liabilities on debt and fiscal sustainability, including the pricing of investment and O&M to ensure life-cycle costing. It should ensure that the public procurement system is integrated into the public financial management system. Weaknesses in infrastructure governance cause inefficiency, making these institutions vulnerable to fraud, corruption, and collusion in the planning, designing, implementation, and management stages. Proper corruption risk assessments and fiduciary due diligence should accompany project processing and implementation and should be monitored during implementation to ensure effectiveness and ongoing quality.[71]

Implementing Principle 6 requires an infrastructure governance framework and the institutional capacity to plan, assess, prioritize, and select projects. The backbone of good infrastructure investments depends on two elements: the enabling environment, like regulations, market structure, competition, and corporate governance and managerial capacity including those of SOEs; and the ability at the project level to select, design, procure, and implement the projects. Projects should be affordable and delivered efficiently, balancing financial and nonfinancial considerations. Infrastructure investments are often politically sensitive and expensive, locking in land use and development paths. It is therefore important that a good governance system identify and assess the costs and benefits of projects, either through cost–benefit analyses, or through cost-effectiveness or multi-criteria analysis, where costs and benefits are hard to monetize. This assessment will provide input for assessing value for money, as described under Principle 2.

Project selection and analysis should follow a national strategic vision and an accompanying infrastructure plan, while specific sector plans specify how to implement this vision. All projects should be subject to consistent and transparent selection criteria based on how they fit government policy priorities, their cost versus benefit, fiscal and debt constraints, vulnerability to corruption, and funding space within the medium-term budget framework. The criteria used to select a project eventually results in an "investment decision" to move ahead with a project or not. Once a government decides that a project is worth procuring, it decides which procurement method— PPP or a more traditional form—is most likely to deliver value for money. Governments should not treat PPP projects differently than other public investment projects; all projects including PPPs should be part of the public investment management plan.

---

70 C. Verzosa and T. Fiutak. 2019. The "How" of Multi-stakeholder Engagement. *ADB Governance Brief*. Manila.

71 Global best practices for integrity in infrastructure procurement are reflected in the 2019 G20 Compendium of Good Practices for Promoting Integrity and Transparency in Infrastructure Development. https://www.oecd.org/g20/summits/osaka/ G20-Compendium-of-Good-Practices-in-Infrastructure-Development.pdf; and the 2015 G20 Principles for Promoting Integrity in Public Procurement. http://g20.org.tr/wp-content/uploads/2015/11/G20-PRINCIPLES-FOR-PROMOTING-INTEGRITY-I N-PUBLIC-PROCUREMENT.pdf.

Infrastructure governance must link the project appraisal process with the budget cycle, even if they have different timetables, as multiyear budgeting can best support project implementation over its life-cycle. Ideally, investment plans should be adequately detailed and realistically formulated in the medium-term expenditure frameworks (MTEFs). MTEFs come from prudent forecasts of available tax and non-tax resources and current spending, allowing for capital spending already in the pipeline, and for adequate levels of spending on operation and maintenance of both existing capital stock and proposed new investments. It is important to analyze different scenarios to determine major risks like contingent liability impact. Debt-financed infrastructure projects and related contingent and direct liabilities should be accounted for in budgets, given the impact of major infrastructure projects on public finance. This will help create better value for money that includes life-cycle costs, increase fiscal sustainability, and ensure fiscal space for future projects. The infrastructure investment decision-making framework must consider both budget and maintenance to ensure efficient resource allocation.

The Asia and Pacific region still has governance and corruption risks. Transparency International reports that countries on average scored 45 out of 100 on its *Corruption Perception Index* in 2020, and the risk of fraud and corruption remains serious and affects infrastructure governance.[72] ADB's governance risk assessment diagnostic informs country partnership strategies, programs, and projects across a broad range of sectors, including infrastructure. The *Second Governance and Anticorruption Action Plan (GACAP II)*[73] is operationalized through selected guidelines, mainly for country- and sector-level governance risk assessments (GRAs), and implemented through several activities and outputs, including risk assessment and management plans (RAMPs), proactive integrity reviews, country portfolio review missions, regular procurement, financial management and anticorruption capacity development, and training events.

RAMPs focus on identifying and responding to risks in three thematic priorities: combating corruption, transparent and competitive procurement, and public financial management. This is also a useful exercise to focus on capacity development interventions and enabling environment policy reforms. The *GACAP II* approach employs RAMPs to assess and make recommendations to improve country systems in DMCs at the national and sector level. RAMPs inform the risks section in country partnership strategies (CPSs), sector strategies and road maps, and project design. Country sector/agency procurement risk assessments provide specific directions on country systems procurement. Risk-based financial management assessments for projects are also prepared.

Infrastructure governance requires sound policy and institutional frameworks across sectors and departments to optimize project preparation decision-making and reduce institutional risks. Figure 16 illustrates the relationship between upstream policy and institutional framework; the drivers of sustainability, efficiency, and accessibility; and the project cycle. Investing in upstream work (public) helps generate downstream transactions supporting the public and private sectors. However, it is hardly a one-off activity. There is a feedback loop that helps governments implement infrastructure governance, linking support for upstream, midstream, and downstream transaction structuring. As noted in the ADB Institute publication *Building the Future of Quality Infrastructure,* planning, project prioritization, and framework risks in traditional and PPP projects result in higher transaction costs that can hinder private investment, contributing to the high price of capital for infrastructure investment even in the current low-rate environment, especially in poor countries.[74]

---

72 Transparency International. 2021. CPI 2020: Asia Pacific. 28 January. https://www.transparency.org/en/news/cpi-2020-asia-pacific.
73 A. Newsum. 2019. Second Governance and Anticorruption Action Plan (GACAP II) Implementation 2006–2018. *ADB Learning Note.* Manila.
74 A. Bhattacharya et al. 2020. *Building the Future of Quality Infrastructure in Policy and Institutional Framework for Delivering on Sustainable Infrastructure.* Tokyo: Asian Development Bank Institute.

Figure 16: Integrating Quality Infrastructure Investment into Upstream Policy and Project Cycle

Business and Policy Environment

QII Principles

Principle 1: Maximizing the Positive Impact of Infrastructure to Achieve Sustainable Growth and Development

Principle 2: Raising Economic Efficiency in View of Life-Cycle Costs

Principle 3: Integrate Environmental Considerations into Projects

Principle 4: Building Resilience Against Natural Disasters and Other Risks

Principle 5: Integrating Social Considerations in Infrastructure Projects

Principle 6: Strengthening Infrastructure Governance

Upstream Policy and Institutional Framework

Sustainability
- ESG, climate and disaster risk assessment, Economic and financial feasibility analysis
- Paris Accord National Determined Contributions
- Whole of government infrastructure planning

Efficiency
- Budgetary governancce fiscal/debt assessments
- Cost-benefit/value for money/life-cycle costing
- Transparent and competitive procurement

Accessibility
- Consulation with stakeholders
- Gender and Marginalized communities
- Users capacity to pay and the use of government subsidies and other fees

Project Cycle

Project Prioritization, Strategic Planning, Screening, and Identification

Project Preparation

Project Structuring

Procurement and tender award

Project Management

Institutional Capacity and Governance

ESG = environment social, and governance; QII = quality infrastructure investment.
Source: Authors.

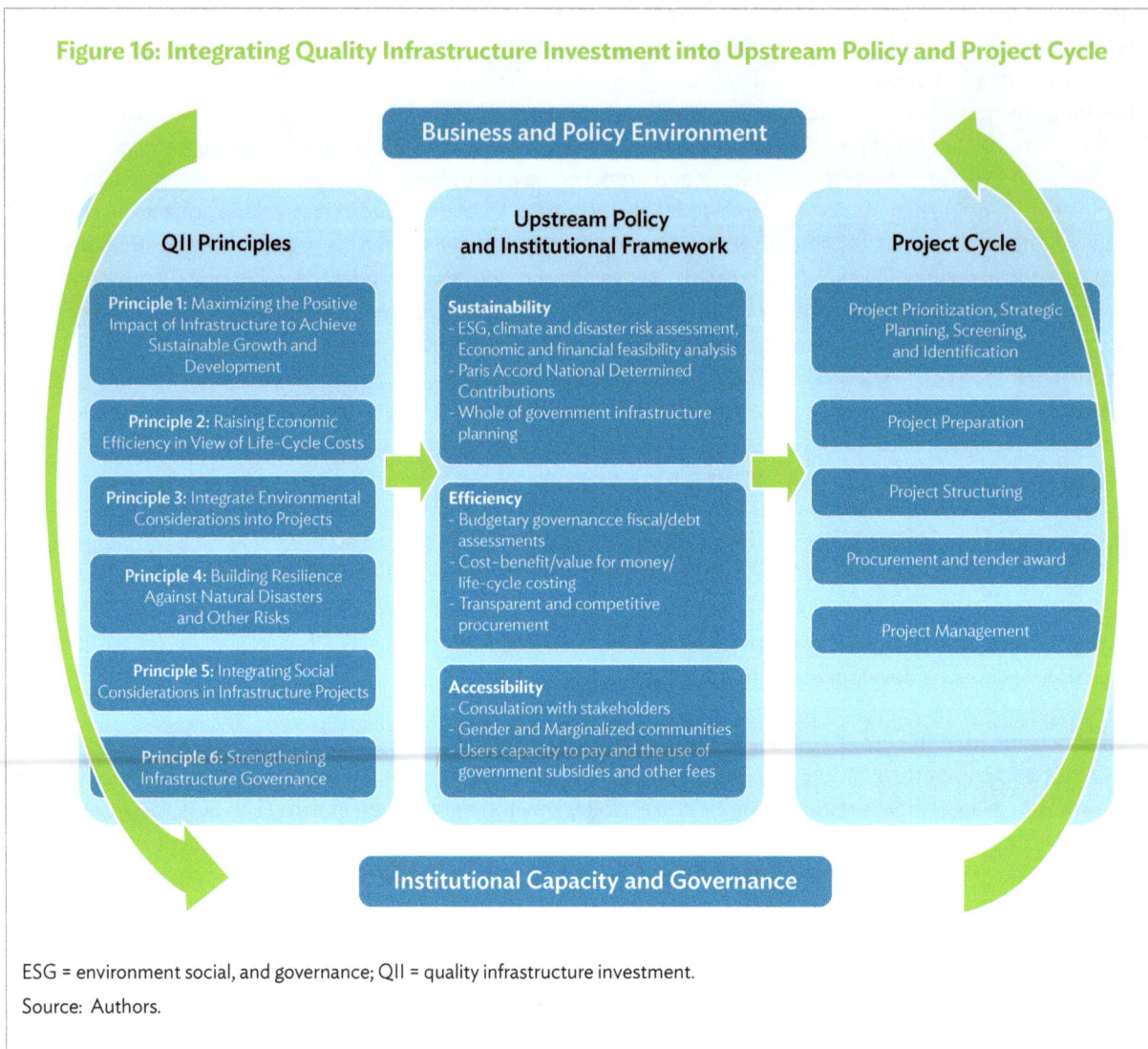

As part of ADB's ongoing work on infrastructure governance and sustainability, the Governance Thematic Group prepared a discussion paper to encourage discussion among ADB staff on risk transfer, especially in PPPs. Questions about the efficacy of VfM and risk transfer in PPPs have contributed to a loss of confidence in PPP transactions in many countries. According to the World Bank, global investment for 2019 was 7% below the previous 5-year average of $103.5 billion. East Asia and the Pacific, mainly led by the PRC, dominated global investments in infrastructure, accounting for 39% of the total; however, this is down from 46% in 2018.[75] The discussion paper argues that a major contributor to this dip in confidence is the approach in PPP contracts regarding risk allocation and dispute resolution (Box 10).

---

[75] See PPIAF Data Base. World Bank (accessed December 2020). https://ppi.worldbank.org/en/ppi.

BOX 10	Risk Allocation Reform and Creating More Collaborative Public–Private Partnerships

Restoring Confidence in Public–Private Partnerships examines alternative contractual arrangements for infrastructure projects and analyzes their suitability for PPPs in development conditions likely to exist following the COVID-19 pandemic.

It considers risk transfer and other factors affecting value for money. These include innovations like alliance contracting, under which parties in a contract make a formal, binding commitment to share risks and rewards under a "no blame" regime. The parties agree on a target cost for the project and transparently share gains and losses if actual costs are more (or less) than the target amount. The paper also examines a number of other collaborative models including a regulatory asset-based approach to monitor the private sector, economic stability clauses for relief in the event of economic hardship, government equity participation in project companies, various forms of early engagements with contractors (such as the "'competitive dialogue" process), and the use of standing dispute boards throughout the life of a PPP project.

The paper also considers various hybrid PPP models used in the Asia and Pacific region. One model is an arrangement where the government develops and finances projects through to the end of the construction phase, followed by the competitive tendering of an operations–maintenance concession. This hybrid model is the essence of the "Build, Build, Build" program initiated by the Government of the Philippines in 2017, under which initiatives such as the Subic–Clark International Airport Expansion and Modernization Project took place. India introduced a similar concept for the road transport sector in the "Toll–Operate–Transfer" (TOT) program, where the National Highways Authority could monetize publicly funded existing toll roads by offering 30-year tolling concessions to private sector operators.

The paper notes that some of the more radical approaches may not be appropriate for PPPs in the Asia and Pacific region. However, it does recommend the consideration of incremental changes to risk allocation arrangements in favor of more collaborative risk sharing to help restore confidence in PPPs among governments and the private sector. The paper also notes that more collaborative approaches to PPPs require higher levels of governance capacity, recommending that, within ADB, the infrastructure, private sector, governance, and procurement departments should work closely together to deliver the required governance capacity-building assistance.

COVID-19 = coronavirus disease, PPP = Public–Private Partnership.
Source: ADB. 2020. *Restoring Confidence in Public–Private Partnerships: Risk Allocation Reform and Creating More Collaborative PPPs*. Manila.

ADB already has an array of project instruments supporting infrastructure governance including technical and institutional knowledge across sectors on strategic infrastructure planning, prioritization, financing, detailed design, implementation, quality control, and operation and maintenance to guide project development based on international best practices. Table 2 shows a selection of these instruments, how they correspond to the QII principles core elements, and how each instrument fits into the infrastructure project cycle.

Table 2: Selected ADB Instruments Related to Quality Infrastructure Investment

ADB Instrument	QII Core element and Principle	Phase in Project Cycle
Safeguard Policy Statement	Sustainable growth and development/ Principle 1 Environmental and social considerations/ Principle 3	Project screening and identification Project preparation
Summary Poverty Reduction and Social Strategy	Sustainable growth and development/ Principle 1	Project screening and identification Project preparation
Guidelines for Economic Analysis	Economic efficiency in view of life-cycle cost/ Principle 2	Project screening and identification Project preparation
Risk-based financial management assessments	Economic efficiency in view of life-cycle cost/ Principle 2	Project screening and identification Project preparation
Climate Risk Management Framework	Building resilience against disasters and other risks/ Principle 4	Project screening and identification Project preparation
Value for Money Guidance on Procurement	Economic efficiency in view of life-cycle cost/ Principle 2 Infrastructure governance/ Principle 6	Project preparation
Environmental Impact Assessment/ Initial Environmental Examination/ Environmental Assessment and Review Framework	Social and environmental impacts/ Principle 3	Project screening and identification Project preparation
Gender Action Plan	Gender/ Principle 5	Project screening and identification Project preparation
Risk Assessment and Risk Management Plan **GACAP II Country- and Sector-level Governance Risk Assessments**	Infrastructure governance/ Principle 6	Project screening and identification Project preparation
Country sector/ agency procurement risk assessments	Economic efficiency in view of life-cycle cost/ Principle 2 Infrastructure governance/ Principle 6	Project screening and identification Project preparation
Corporate Results Framework	Infrastructure governance/ Principle 6	Project preparation Project management
Proactive Integrity Review	Infrastructure governance/ Principle 6	Project evaluation

ADB = Asian Deelopment Bank, GACAP = Governance and Anticorruption Action Plan, QII = quality infrastructure invesment.

Source: Author.

ADB's evaluation document, ADB Support for Public–Private Partnerships (2009–2019), also highlights the need to strengthen upstream policy support and the enabling environment. The evaluation calls for a more consistent engagement at an early stage to screen and select projects for public, PPP, and other modes of procurement using cost-benefit and VfM analyses to help governments improve the quality of PPP project structuring and delivery (Box 11).

BOX 11   **Evaluating ADB Support for Public–Private Partnerships (2009–2019)**

Asian Development Bank (ADB) support for public–private partnerships (PPPs) and the relevance of the *Public–Private Partnership Operational Plan 2012–2020*, the performance and results of ADB support for PPPs, and organizational issues affecting ADB's PPP support during the period 2009–2019 are assessed in the context of *Strategy 2030*. The thematic evaluation seeks to understand the best response to the demand for PPP policy or transaction advisory work and investment opportunities across different sectors and countries. It reviews technical assistance support and transaction advisory services to sovereign and nonsovereign PPP interventions in larger developing member countries (DMCs) and smaller frontier markets. The overall aim is to understand how ADB can best leverage PPP knowledge, risk appetite, and financial resources to deliver optimal development outcomes.

The evaluation found that ADB's PPP operational plan did not have clear performance measures and lacked focus on promoting advocacy, capacity development, and the PPP enabling environment. This led to an unclear allocation of roles and responsibilities across the PPP delivery chain. The evaluation recommends ADB prepare and implement a new PPP strategy and update the operational plan to increase the focus on capacity development and the PPP enabling environment, in line with Strategy 2030's operational priorities and quality infrastructure outcomes.

ADB support for PPPs has not been engaged consistently at an early stage to screen and select projects for public, PPP, and other modes of procurement using cost–benefit and value for money analysis. The evaluation recommends that ADB proactively engage governments of DMCs from an early stage to help them review multiple possible infrastructure procurement options.

The evaluation notes that financing availability is not the major hurdle in delivering PPP infrastructure projects in DMCs; managing and appropriately pricing project risks to raise private capital resources is the challenge. PPP market participants would highly value more risk products like partial risk and credit guarantees and blended finance interventions. ADB should increase the scale and scope of risk mitigation products including the offering of political risk and partial credit guarantees.

ADB's current PPP monitoring system and transaction databases are unsuited to the task of monitoring the full scope of ADB's PPP interventions. The evaluation calls for an improvement in ADB monitoring and evaluation systems covering long-term outcomes beyond project closure, commercial close, and operational maturity.

Source: ADB. 2020. *ADB Support for Public–Private Partnerships (2009–2019)*. Independent Evaluation Office.

SECTION
7

ASSESSMENT AND PERFORMANCE OF QUALITY INFRASTRUCTURE INVESTMENT

The Corporate Results Framework and the ADF 13th Replenishment uphold the key elements of quality infrastructure dealing with climate change, building climate and disaster resilience, and enhancing environmental sustainability (OP3), and accelerating gender equality (ADB Operational Priority 2). Quality infrastructure also supports the goal of OP3 to scale climate change and disaster risk activities to address climate change, disaster risks, and environmental degradation; invest in green economic growth; and improve access to smarter technologies.

ADB supports infrastructure projects that offer opportunities for women in skilled jobs and increase access to markets. The ADF 13 Donors Report states that 100% of the infrastructure projects supported by ADF 13 will incorporate "G20 Principles for Quality Infrastructure Investment" as measured using the 2019–2024 corporate results framework indicator "operations that are green, sustainable, inclusive, and resilient." The report upholds the importance of life-cycle costs; sustainability, including debt sustainability and transparency; and resilience and inclusivity in infrastructure investment.

QII principles are too broad for operational purposes. From a governance perspective, the most relevant pillars of the Corporate Results Framework (CRF) to QII is OP6 for strengthening governance and institutional capacity. The principles align with the ADB consolidated results framework indicators for OP6 of Strategy 2030 regarding the priority of strengthening institutional capacity and governance to improve public sector management functions and financial stability.[76] QII principles also relate to ADB's *Corporate Results Framework, 2019–2024*, particularly for governance (Table 3).

---

[76] ADB. 2018. *Strategy 2030: Governance and Anticorruption Action Plan*. Manila.

Table 3: ADB Corporate Results Framework, 2019–2024

Pillar 1: Improved public and corporate sector management functions and financial stability	Pillar 2: More effective, timely, corruption-free, and citizen-centric delivery of services
◗ Entities with improved management functions and financial stability (number) ◗ Government officials with increased capacity to design, implement, monitor, and evaluate relevant measures (number) ◗ Measures supported in implementation to improve capacity of public organizations to promote the private sector and finance sector (number) ◗ Measures supported in implementation that promote resilience and responsiveness to economic shocks in a timely manner (number) ◗ Transparency and accountability measures in procurement and financial management supported in implementation (number)	◗ Entities with improved service delivery (number) ◗ Service delivery standards adopted and/or supported in implementation by government and/or private entities (number) ◗ Measures supported in implementation to strengthen subnational entities' ability to better manage their public finances (number) ◗ Measures to strengthen SOE governance supported in implementation (number) ◗ Citizen engagement mechanisms adopted (number)

ADB = Asian Development Bank, SOE = state-owned enterprise.

Source: ADB. 2019. *Corporate Results Framework, 2019–2024.*

ADB and other multilateral institutions have developed various metrics of sustainability and performance. It is also important to identify metrics upstream when governments develop project pipelines to assess gaps in infrastructure governance and provide technical assistance to help DMCs address these gaps. ADB's Strategy, Policy and Partnerships Department (SPD) developed a tracking indicator on quality infrastructure included in ADB's Strategy 2030 corporate results framework. ADB's green, resilient, inclusive, and sustainable (GRIS) indicator is a composite index of qualitative criteria related to the four principles of quality infrastructure in Strategy 2030 and is in the investment approval stage.

GRIS also focuses on promoting gender equality and action on climate change and reinforces for G20 QII principles aimed at improving financial sustainability and encouraging life-cycle costing. GRIS was applied to ADB projects in the energy, water, and transport sector approved in 2019, with the results reported in the 2019 *Development Effectiveness Review* published in April 2020. SPD has revised the indicator and is integrating it into the SOURCE software platform to support its operationalization at a country level.[77] While SOURCE templates include the GRIS indicator, they can be revised to support other indicators like future QII indicators, approved by the multilateral development banks overseeing the template revisions.

The World Bank is developing an infrastructure governance tool to assess gaps and recommend reforms. The tool will evaluate the quality of infrastructure governance at the country level, benchmark performance against international good practices among peer groups, identify serious gaps, and prioritize reform interventions. This is in line with the IDA commitment to undertake this assessment in at least 20 countries during IDA19, focusing on countries needing to improve their performance based on the World Bank's Country Policy and Institutional Assessment indicator 16, which covers corruption, transparency, and accountability. This commitment will help IDA

---

[77] SOURCE is a digital project preparation platform designed to improve project quality based on international best practices developed in consultation with the private sector, multilateral development banks, and international organizations. It also serves as repository of the latest tools and diagnostics related to infrastructure project preparation.

countries identify the major governance bottlenecks in infrastructure investments through better diagnostics that help inform policies and/or regulations to address them.[78]

The GIF, a global project preparation platform, has incorporated QII principles into the GIF portfolio results framework for project preparation activities. The project-level indicators are aggregated at the portfolio level and include support for the implementation of VfM, climate mitigation, and fiscal impact. This GIH Reference Guide considers PPP models and demonstrates how output and outcome indicators are used to measure the quality of infrastructure. The ability of infrastructure like hydroelectric dams to stand up to natural hazards is a project outcome and is based on project output requiring a minimum capacity to withstand seismic activity.[79]

Greater upstream engagement for the policy and regulatory environment and midstream in the infrastructure project cycle will help ensure VfM, life-cycle costing, fiscal and institutional sustainability, and improved investment efficiency. ADB has made good progress in implementing safeguards, results frameworks, and climate policy support. Based on recent sector evaluations for energy and transport PPPs, ADB needs to place more focus on upstream activities to support enabling environments, capacity development, and sector planning. ADB can use its expertise, financial resources, and policy dialogue to promote effective infrastructure planning and public sector management capacity that will generate higher impact investment opportunities. This will be particularly important as countries emerge from the pandemic; DMCs will likely seek essential policy advice and financial and institutional support to restore their economic growth.

Project preparation technical assistance should include quality infrastructure components, ensure tracking and monitoring of investment activities, incorporate infrastructure governance indicators into existing results frameworks, and disseminate knowledge on how improved infrastructure governance results in better project and portfolio outcomes. Technical assistance should build institutional capacity in DMCs to improve economic efficiency of investments based on assessments of life-cycle costs and VfM. ADB already includes environmental and social sustainability, green investment, and building climate and disaster resilience under Strategy 2030. Quality infrastructure investment will not only help in "building back better" after COVID-19, but also contribute to achieving economic efficiencies, closing the infrastructure gap, and promoting sustainable growth.

Implementing improved infrastructure governance in DMCs requires sophistication in government contracting authorities to plan, procure, and manage infrastructure projects. It also requires strengthened collaboration among thematic groups, departments with relevant knowledge, and regional departments within ADB. In addition, it requires additional capacity in government fiscal authorities to enable refined calculations of liabilities and other contingencies, and the ability to assess the cost of project risks and establish a consistent methodology for applying VfM and life-cycle costing to infrastructure projects. The level of governance capacity needed for infrastructure investment presents a challenge and an opportunity for multilateral and bilateral development agencies, and transparency and accountability remain critically important. These are attainable by strengthening the understanding of contracting agencies in how to implement improved infrastructure governance.

To accomplish this, ADB needs to coordinate its technical assistance and capacity-building programs for PPP units, finance officials, and infrastructure line ministries. ADB and other multilateral agency support for capacity building is critical as a counterpart to transactional support. Upstream support by ADB to build local capacity should not be a one-time operation. Government officials change and new ideas emerge. The recent evaluation

78   International Development Association (IDA). 2020. *Additions to IDA Resources: Nineteenth Replenishment. IDA 19: Ten Years to 2030: Growth, People, Resilience.* Washington, DC: World Bank Group.
79   Global Infrastructure Hub (GIH). 2019. *Reference Guide on Output Specifications for Quality Infrastructure.* Australia.

of PPP support revealed the importance of a "One ADB" approach—close coordination and a feedback loop between transaction experience and upstream and mid-stream policy and capacity building. The infrastructure, private sector, governance, public procurement, and financial management departments of ADB need to work together to help contracting authorities develop the requisite skills.

Quality infrastructure governance recommendations to support sustainable recovery and deliver key policy priorities are more critical post-COVID. While COVID-19 has caused a health, economic, and social crisis, it also underscored the need to do things differently, mainstreaming "green recovery" in the project cycle and greater collaboration regionally and with development partners to innovate and to "build back better." With this in mind, ADB should

- **Adopt a "One ADB" approach to quality infrastructure:** ADB's Strategy 2030 recognizes the thematic approach, where the focus is on integrating sector work in themes and ensuring cross-cutting initiatives. Quality infrastructure requires expertise and knowledge in a range of areas to address governance and development challenges and to develop integrated solutions. To assist DMCs in developing high levels of governance capacity, ADB needs to ensure that its technical assistance programs—for traditional infrastructure and PPP units, finance officials, procurement authorities, and infrastructure line ministries—are closely linked. Bridging internal departments of development agencies will be critical in developing a more collaborative approach.

- **Embed infrastructure governance in the country partnership strategy:** Infrastructure projects are complex, requiring upstream planning, project prioritization, sound frameworks for procurement of traditional and PPP projects, institutional capacities for public financial management and governance, and a sound business and policy environment. To have maximum impact, an integrated infrastructure governance assessment at the CPS level is required, informed by a guidance note on infrastructure governance to support ADB in preparing a strategic long-term vision for infrastructure and sector-based policies in DMCs. It should address infrastructure governance in an integrated fashion where authorities plan, procure, deliver, fund, and finance infrastructure while ensuring that long-term infrastructure plans are fiscally sustainable. It should consider transparency, stakeholder participation, and capacity to manage threats to integrity. The note should draw upon existing ADB knowledge products and develop infrastructure governance diagnostic tools to serve as an input into the country dialogue.

- **Integrate ADB diagnostic instruments:** Infrastructure investment is characterized by increasing levels of complexity to meet multiple objectives and deliver multiple benefits in the short and long term, within the context of increasingly interconnected and interdependent infrastructure systems across geographies, sectors, and levels of government. ADB has an array of instruments/filters that correspond to infrastructure governance. The challenge is integrating stand-alone instruments cohesively to address economic, social, fiscal, environmental, and climate-related costs and benefits and account for the full life-cycle of the infrastructure assets. Further refinements of country diagnostic assessments need to be tailored to meet individual country circumstances for implementing infrastructure governance in alignment with national-level policy priorities and long-term development goals.

- **Embrace programmatic approaches to infrastructure governance at national and subnational levels:** ADB should build on programmatic approaches to quality infrastructure to support reforms through policy-based lending, support smaller scale investments through results-based lending, and finally through infrastructure investment projects. It will be critical to strengthen the ability of DMCs to identify and manage infrastructure risks at the institutional level, especially in subnational entities. National-level support for subnational infrastructure investment plays a critical role in investing in sustainable and resilient infrastructure. All levels of government and institutions need to closely coordinate to ensure timely investment to support post-COVID-19 recovery the quality of infrastructure investments. This requires improved capacity to monitor and evaluate the quality of infrastructure governance at the intermediate levels of government—regions, states, provinces—and should be part of national investment recovery strategies and dialogue with country authorities to prepare the ADB CPS.

⊙ **Provide upstream and midstream support to improve infrastructure governance:** Realizing value for money across the life-cycle of infrastructure assets requires a greater focus on upstream and midstream institutional capacity to strengthen public investment efficiency of DMCs. In providing technical assistance to build capacity in DMCs, ADB should focus more on upstream and midstream planning, project selection, preparation, and fiscal and debt management, and downstream monitoring and evaluation. This includes supporting DMCs to adopt the necessary policy and regulatory frameworks providing the enabling conditions, incentives, and standards to promote sustainable infrastructure investment. It also includes ensuring strong governance mechanisms so that the right infrastructure gets built cost effectively and affordably, with the approval and support of stakeholders.

Capacity-building support for infrastructure governance needs more integrated and holistic support across ministries for planning, selecting projects, budgeting, and managing infrastructure contracts and risks. It also requires systemic engagement and capacity building beyond the narrow confines of a single project. Moreover, infrastructure investment depends on fiscal authorities' capacity to implement sound public financial management to ensure fiscal and debt sustainability. This requires a greater focus on ensuring that authorities link the plans with budget allocations in alignment with medium-term expenditure frameworks. A robust, transparent, and accountable capital budgeting framework will help build trust in government and meet national development needs cost-effectively and coherently.

⊙ **Mobilize private finance through risk sharing and mitigation:** Financing for quality, sustainable infrastructure needs to be significantly scaled-up to support a strong, inclusive, and green recovery from COVID-19. Given increasing budget pressures, governments need to mobilize private finance to complement public investment. To broaden the investor base, appropriate capital market instruments and vehicles for channeling financing for infrastructure projects must be available so that institutional investors can invest without undue regulatory constraints. The perception of policy, regulatory, and institutional risks in DMCs have limited the extent of institutional investment in DMCs. Risk perception by institutional investors in a post-COVID world is likely to continue given the increased debt and fiscal pressure, especially in poorer countries.

Carefully calibrated government intervention can influence the risk profile of infrastructure investments by influencing the overall level of risk, managing environmental and social risks, and promoting diversified risk mitigation instruments and incentives. ADB addresses this challenge by utilizing private sector resources for PPPs and providing specialized infrastructure financial products like blended finance, equity, and guarantees. ADB's commitment to climate financing and innovative green bonds also strengthens the financing market for green investments. Expanding the pool of private finance by mitigating public and private stakeholder risks and enhanced policy dialogue with DMCs and the private sector to improve infrastructure governance are essential in meeting strategic investment needs. ADB also can help increase private finance by promoting infrastructure as an asset class—for example, by improving DMCs' ability to measure and maintain data on the historical performance of infrastructure assets.

○ **Improve infrastructure governance for traditional investments and PPPs:** Countries need to improve oversight of traditional investment projects and PPPs and to integrate economic efficiency, environmental and social sustainability, adaption, and resiliency into the operational framework of sustainable infrastructure development. The PPP thematic evaluation noted the need for more focus on capacity development and the enabling environment, aligned with pillars one and two of ADB's PPP Operational Plan 2012–2020. The evaluation found that upstream work was mainly focused on sovereign interventions through policy-based loans and TA projects promoting advocacy, capacity development, and targeted support for the PPP enabling environment.

Effective infrastructure governance also requires looking beyond the planning and prioritization process and ensuring that infrastructure endures over the asset life-cycle. This requires monitoring strategies, paying due consideration to the operation and maintenance of infrastructure assets, and fostering investments to reinforce the resilience of infrastructure systems. DMCs should strengthen the oversight of PPP units to ensure that PPP contract performance is adequately monitored and evaluated. Strengthening the governance and performance of economic regulators also supports the market efficiency, quality, reliability, and affordability of private infrastructure services and ensures the provision of critical infrastructure services following COVID-19.

○ **Use technology and innovation to improve infrastructure governance:** The infrastructure sector is behind other sectors in the adaptation and implementation of innovative technologies even after recognizing the potential transformative role of infrastructure technology across industries. AI/machine learning and big data can pave the way for adaption of smart city technologies and management by making transportation and the built environment more intelligent and energy efficient. Big data can monitor the pandemic impact on traffic patterns and transport patterns.

Technology can also improve infrastructure governance. This should emphasize the extensive use of digital platforms in progress monitoring, and troubleshooting mechanisms operating in real-time to pursue better governance and implementation. SOURCE is a platform which digitizes infrastructure project preparation and data collection, thereby supporting better governance and implementation discipline while disseminating ADB tools, safeguards, and other knowledge products related to improving infrastructure governance. Making relevant ADB tools and diagnostics more widely accessible to DMCs has the potential to promote interest and understanding of issues around infrastructure governance. DMC demand for ADB technical assistance may also increase to support the use of these tools and knowledge products.

○ **Collaborate with development partners:** Infrastructure governance depends on country leadership and policy vision to improve the efficiency in how DMCs identify, plan, design, and allocate resources. ADB can expand existing collaboration with the IMF, for example, to conduct PIMA diagnostics to identify infrastructure governance gaps. Building a common understanding of the importance of infrastructure governance among decision makers is necessary for its successful implementation.

The IMF, OECD, World Bank, JICA, and other development bodies are crucial knowledge partners for ADB in improving DMC understanding and implementation of sustainable, low-carbon, inclusive, quality infrastructure objectives. Cofinancing from partners can also help alleviate the initial costs of implementing infrastructure governance borne by DMCs. The various departments within multilateral and bilateral development agencies dealing with infrastructure, private sector development, governance, and public procurement also need to work together, coordinating and intensifying their existing programs, to help governments in emerging and developing markets acquire the requisite skills.